An Important Message to Our Readers

This product provides information and general advice about the law. But laws and procedures change frequently, and they can be interpreted differently by different people. For specific advice geared to your specific situation, consult an expert. No book, software or other published material is a substitute for personalized advice from a knowledgeable lawyer licensed to practice law in your state.

1st edition

How to Get Your
Business
on the Web

A Legal Guide to E-Commerce

by Attorney Fred Steingold

Keeping Up-to-Date

To keep its books up-to-date, Nolo issues new printings and new editions periodically. New printings reflect minor legal changes and technical corrections. New editions contain major legal changes, major text additions or major reorganizations. To find out if a later printing or edition of any Nolo book is available, call Nolo at 510-549-1976 or check our website at http://www.nolo.com.

To stay current, follow the "Update" service at our website at http://www.nolo.com/update. In another effort to help you use Nolo's latest materials, we offer a 35% discount off the purchase of the new edition of your Nolo book when you turn in the cover of an earlier edition. (See the "Special Upgrade Offer" in the back of the book.) This book was last revised in January 2002.

1st Edition	JANUARY 2002
Editor	RICHARD STIM
Book Design & Production	SUSAN PUTNEY
Illustrations	SASHA STIM-VOGEL
Index	JULIE SHAWVAN
Proofreading	ROBERT WELLS
Printing	BERTELSMANN SERVICES, INC.

Steingold, Fred.
   How to get your business on the Web : a legal guide to e-commerce / by Fred S. Steingold.
        p.   cm.
   Includes index.
   ISBN 0-87337-753-2
     1. Electronic commerce--Law and legislation–United States--Popular works. 2. Internet--Law and legislation–United States--Popular works. I. Title

KF390.5.C6 S74 2001
343.73'07--dc21   2001044020

For information on bulk purchases or corporate premium sales, please contact the Special Sales Department. For academic sales or textbook adoptions, ask for Academic Sales. Call 800-955-4775 or write to Nolo, 950 Parker Street, Berkeley, CA 94710.

Acknowledgements

I wish to thank the many members of the Nolo family who helped make this book a reality, with special thanks to:

- Founder Jake Warner and Publisher Janet Portman who encouraged me to proceed with this challenging project, and

- Editors Mary Randolph and Rich Stim who skillfully shaped the final product.

Thanks too, to the following people who generously provided information and insights for this book: David Bloom, Ron Fisher, Timothy Fort, Nina Howard, Michael Kismal, Susan Kornfield, Toby Levin, Valerie Mates, Toni Morrell, Thomas Reynolds, Charles Rice, Kurt Riegger, Chris Rizik, Tom Root, Peter Scheer, Carol Shepherd, David and Dennis Singsank, and Sarah Veit.

Table of Contents

1 What Type of Online Business Are You?

2 Choosing and Protecting Your Domain Name

3 Creating Your Website

What Type of Online Business Are You?

So you have a small business—or are about to start one—and you'd like to have a presence on the Web. Well, online certainly is the place to be and this book will show you, step by step, how to get there.

You'll find an abundance of practical information here about how business is conducted on the Internet. But, equally important, we've also tried to foresee the common legal issues that can arise when you bring your business online. So with this book at hand, your trips to a lawyer's office should be few and far between, although we do tell you when getting a lawyer's advice is crucial.

Keep in mind that as your website gets more complex and as you reach out to a broader market to sell your goods, services and information, the potential for legal problems increases. This book will help you keep those legal problems to a minimum.

Although the dot-com bubble has burst for many "pure" Internet businesses—websites that profited primarily from Internet advertising—the demise of these businesses has had little effect on small businesses on the Web. By mid-2001, the International Data Corp. reported that almost three-quarters of small businesses with PCs were on the Internet.

How effective is the Web for a small business? According to a Verizon study published at the end of 2000, 55% of small business that go online either break even or completely pay for their website with increased business within one year. In addition, 48% of online businesses report an increase in customers within a 50-mile radius compared to only 20% of offline businesses. Also encouraging according to Verizon was the fact that 57% of small businesses felt that setting up a website was easy. (For more Internet statistics, check InternetStats.com (http://www.internetstats.com))

It's hard to think of a business that wouldn't benefit from being accessible on the Web. Even a one-person operation can bolster its image and profits merely by posting a website where people can go for information about what the business offers and how to contact the owner.

But that's just the beginning. Many small businesses can reap greater rewards by having more sophisticated, interactive sites. If you wish, you can create a website where customers can order products, communicate with your company (or each other), sign up for services, download information and link to other sites. The potential for being creative and building a profitable business through the Internet is enormous.

To illustrate the range of small business websites, from simple online advertisements to complex sites that sell products and provide message boards or chat rooms, this chapter details some real-life examples of creative, successful sites. We hope one or more of them inspires you to build a great website.

A. The Advertisement: valeriemates.com

SUMMARY: *Passive site that provides information about the company's services.*

Like many a budding entrepreneur, programmer Valerie Mates had had her fill of working for a large corporate employer. One day, with little money in the bank but an abundance of self-confidence, she fled the corporate nest and set up her own home-based consulting business. She's never looked back. Her business was successful from the start.

Valerie offered two kinds of services: Web page design and a specialized kind of computer work called Common Gateway Interface (CGI) programming. (CGI has to do with those boxes on the screen where consumers fill in information.) There was a definite market for the kind of services that Valerie provided, and she could work at home in her basement office.

In the early days, Valerie used the Web to find tutorials that helped her hone her already impressive technical skills. She also used the Web to find potential clients. Then, after a few years, she created her own informational site. It has only one interactive feature: a storytelling

program that visitors can download and use for their personal entertainment. The rest of the site simply gives prospective clients a way to know Valerie a bit better.

If Valerie is bidding on a job, she will direct visitors to the pages on her site that show projects for other clients. She also includes her URL in her email signature so that anyone she corresponds with can click on the link and see her site. Others find her site using search engines or links back from websites she has worked on. Valerie has also authored a freeware program that creates links all over the Net. It's become quite popular, and hundreds of other website owners have downloaded it to use in connection with their websites. (For information on it, visit her site.)

Visitors to Valerie's site can learn something about the services she offers, how she does business, what kind of person she is and even her philosophy of life. Her personality definitely shines through. The site is also a showcase for her Web page design work. Visitors can click through to some of the sites she's created and see exactly what she's done.

Valerie sees her site as a sophisticated brochure that is easily accessible to potential clients and has more depth than a traditional paper-and-ink brochure might have. As a Web page expert, Valerie obviously is well aware of the merits of more interactive sites, but for her one-person business, an informational site works just fine.

B. The Information Center: bellanina.com

SUMMARY: *Primarily a passive site with information about the company's services and products. Consumers can also purchase several items.*

What could be further removed from the high-tech world than a massage and beauty business? Yet, facial massage specialist Nina Howard, with help from some local technical specialists, has been able to create a site and prosper from it. Nina is also an artist who works with acrylic painting and does interior design. After working for 12 years in New York City as an employee of an interior design firm, Nina decided it was time to strike out on her own. She moved to a Midwest college town where she rented a house in the historic district. She lived in part of the house and used the rest as an art studio and a place to perform facial massages. Relying solely on a sign in the window ("Nina Howard Studio") and word-of-mouth, her business grew. After a year or so, she decided to live elsewhere so she could use the house entirely for her business. The following year, Nina hired her first employee—a massage therapist—to help carry the workload. She also began carrying skin care products as a convenience to her clients.

Nina's business continued to grow. Her business morphed into "Nina Howard Studio and Day Spa." And she began training other people in the facial massage technique she uses, frequently traveling to other cities to perform the training. The newly minted massage therapists needed skin care products for their work and for their own clients, and Nina was happy to supply them.

Then Nina got the bright idea of going online. It was a simple concept at first. She'd have a website where she could display her catalog of skin care products for her students and former students to purchase. She hired a local website designer to create the site for her. At first, it was just an informational site where people could see descriptions of the products. Customers would call, email or fax orders.

After a year and a half of being online, Nina made her site interactive by adding a simple shopping cart feature. Customers could now order products directly online, and Nina would ship them out. Ordering became much more convenient for Nina and her customers. About this time, Nina decided to change the name of her business to Bellanina Day Spa and Gift Boutique, and her website domain name to http://www.bellanina.com. The new name was an inspired choice, reflecting the fact that her business focuses on beauty. It also harks back to Nina's childhood days when she had the nickname Ninabel.

Nina expanded traffic to her site by having the five manufacturers she deals with provide links to her site from theirs. Someone looking to buy a particular brand of skin care product might start at the manufacturer's site, but then click a link to the Bellanina site and place an order there.

In the first six months that she was online, fully 25% of her sales came from the Internet, and that percentage has continued to increase. Her overall business has grown to the point where she now has ten employees. And she has found additional uses for her website. For example, she offers gift certificates and gift baskets, displays her artwork online and also promotes rental of a vacation home she owns in the Smoky Mountains.

What does the future hold? Perhaps an online newsletter for informing clients and customers of monthly specials and a book section featuring books on health and beauty, with book orders fulfilled by a major online bookseller. She may also add a line of greeting cards featuring her own work as an acrylic artist and photographer.

Incidentally, when she started her business, Nina had trouble getting bankers and other investors to take her seriously. So she financed her budding business by a method known to many an eager entrepreneur—judicious use of several credit cards.

C. The Store: zingermans.com

SUMMARY: *Interactive site with an extensive inventory and state-of-the-art shopping cart features. Detailed product and gourmet information; an online counterpart to a brick-and-mortar store.*

Can a one-location, corner deli benefit from having a website? *Absolutely.* Zingerman's Delicatessen has done just that. From the day in 1982 when founders Ari Weinzweig and Paul Saginaw opened the deli on a corner in Ann Arbor, Michigan, Zingerman's (a name the founders made up) has built a loyal following among foodlovers. Shoppers return again and again to experience the mouth-watering sight, smell and taste of quality foods—meats, cheeses, fish, salads, breads, pastries, olive oils, chocolates, teas and much, much more. The founders built a successful business by sticking to their mantra: "Great food! Great Service! Great Finance!"

Along the way, they've branched out into related businesses, all related to food and all bearing the distinctive look and feel of Zingerman's Deli. For example, Zingerman's Bakehouse produces the breads that the deli uses in its sandwiches, and also sells breads and pastries directly to individuals and through local markets. Zingerman's Catering provides food and service to customers off the premises. And Zingerman's Mail Order ships food that people order from the Zingerman's Catalog.

In 1999, Toni Morell (a Zingerman's manager) and her friend Tom Root (a technology wizard) put together a plan for a Zingerman's website. Their vision soon became a reality when http:// www.zingermans.com (no apostrophe) was created. Zingermans.com is a separate legal entity—specifically, a limited liability company—owned partly by Toni and Tom and partly by the parent Zingerman's company. Take a look at the website and you'll instantly see the unique Zingerman's personality come alive on your screen.

Since Zingerman's places a high value on customer service—it's part of their mantra, remember—they felt they needed more than a passive, informational site. So they developed a friendly interactive site where customers can order everything in the Zingerman's Catalog and some other products as well. And they put synergy to work. Zingermans.com maintains no inventory or shipping facilities. The orders are filled by Zingerman's Mail Order.

The website has been a convenience to thousands of Zingerman's fans, and sales have been strong. Toni and Tom wisely elected not to automate the operation completely, even though it would have been more efficient to do so. Toni personally reviews each order before it's sent along to be filled. She says that customers often make mistakes in an order or are not clear in stating their wishes. When that happens, the customer receives a phone call from Toni to set things right. And customers themselves can call the business, or communicate by fax or email. Nothing stand-offish about this site.

Because of Tom's technical skills, the site hasn't had to use a Web host. (Web hosting is discussed in Chapter 4.) All the necessary equipment is kept in the zingermans.com offices. The site did require some outside help, however, in building digital "firewalls" so that customer data could be kept private in credit card transactions. Also, although a Zingerman's Deli staffer handled most of the site's graphics, a bit of outside art consultation was needed.

Toni and Tom have proved that you don't have to be a huge company to have a first-class website. Both *U.S. News & World Report* and *Forbes* have picked zingermans.com as a top food site.

D. The Store and More: eKnitting.com

SUMMARY: *Interactive site with extensive inventory, detailed product information, state-of-the-art shopping cart features and community atmosphere complete with message boards and links to knitting clubs. Online counterpart to a brick-and-mortar store, also named "eKnitting.com," which opened after the website began.*

Sarah Veit graduated from business school in 1999. After a few months of job searching, she decided to create an online business around her love of knitting. Using her business school knowledge, she prepared a business plan and sought financing primarily from family and friends.

Sarah designed the site with the help of a website development company, Beck In-

teractive, based in nearby San Carlos, California. "I know a lot about knitting," says Sarah, "and they knew a lot about website technology. Together we created the site. What I liked about working with them is that they were receptive to learning about knitting and they incorporated that knowledge into making a unique site."

During the website development process, Sarah looked at other sites to get ideas. One thing that Sarah thought would work was to provide a forum for customers to discuss knitting—the eKnitting.com community. "The community was created for two reasons," says Sarah. "First, it made sense because knitting is by nature a community oriented activity, but also because at the time we created the site, a lot of people were talking about "stickiness" (the ability of a site to retain visitors) and getting loyalty to the site. I thought if people could think of us as a community, there was a higher probability that they would buy from us. I have found that to be the case."

Sarah also decided to open a store in Berkeley. She believed that the store would increase the site's credibility by giving it a real world and a virtual presence. She also felt that the physical store and the online store would complement each other. For example, she sells miscellaneous items and remainders from her online store as odds and ends at the Berkeley store. ∎

CHAPTER

2

Choosing and Protecting Your Domain Name

To do business on the Web, you'll need at least one domain name—an online address that lets people get to your website. This chapter explains how to pick a domain name that won't conflict with someone else's, or with another company's trademark. Also, it tells you how to register your domain name, and protect it as a trademark.

A. Choosing Your Domain Name

You're already aware that a domain name looks like this: *www.protobiz.com*. The letters *www* (World Wide Web) are automatically a part of every domain name. The middle part—*protobiz* in our example—is the unique name that you select and register for your business.

When it comes to the last part of a domain name—*.com*, in our example—there are currently (October 2001) eight choices:

- .com, for commercial enterprises
- .edu, for educational institutions
- .gov, for governmental agencies
- .net, for network-related entities
- .org, for nonprofit organizations
- .biz, for businesses
- .info, for information providers, and
- .name, for individuals.

The Internet Corporation for Assigned Names and Numbers (ICANN), the agency that oversees domain name procedures, has approved four more suffixes, which should be available by the end of 2001. They are:

- .pro, for professionals, such as accountants, lawyers and physicians
- .museum, for museums
- .aero, for the air-transport industry, and
- .coop, for business cooperatives.

For up-to-date information about their status, go to http://www.icann.org/tlds.

Keep in mind that the guidelines for many of these suffixes are not strictly enforced. For example, anyone can acquire a .com, .net, .org, .biz or .info domain name regardless of the type of business they operate. But strictly enforced standards put the .edu and .gov suffixes beyond your reach. Similarly, the .name extension is for individuals, not businesses. When .coop, .aero, .museum and .pro become available, their use will also be restricted—for example, an .aero registration will be issued only to a business in the air-transport industry.

Most businesses in this country have chosen a .com designation. In fact, registrations for .coms have outpaced any other by ten to one. While it's dangerous to predict the future, many observers believe that the preference for .com will continue even after the new options finally become available. Rightly or wrongly, business people seem to feel that the .com designation provides familiarity to consumers and confers an extra measure of prestige on the business using it.

You can register under several suffixes—for example, *protobiz.com, protobiz.net* and *protobiz.org*. That would keep other businesses from registering *protobiz* as part of a domain name with any of those suffixes. When someone types any of these domain names into a browser, your domain name registrar should be able to direct that visitor to your site.

Country Codes & Non-Standard Suffixes

In addition to the .com, .org and other suffixes, there are other less common suffixes available including country code suffixes such as .uk and .dk, and non-ICANN suffixes such as .kids and .tech.

Every country has a country code. For example, the country code suffix for the United States is *.us*. For France it's *.fr* and for Greece it's *.gr*. The rules for obtaining one of these vary from country to country. Your business may qualify for a country code suffix even if it's not physically present in that country. Still, almost all U.S. businesses (and most other places as well) prefer a generic suffix such as .com.

Occasionally, a business will choose a country code because the letters have some supposed promotional value. For example, the country code for Tuvalu is .tv, making it possible to acquire www.comedy.tv as a domain name. Similarly, the country code for Moldova is .md, so a doctor can nail down www.johnsmith.md. The country code for Andorra is .ad, making it a popular choice for commercial advertising businesses.

For now, the use of country codes is considered a novelty, outside mainstream business practice. In addition, many nations place additional burdens on registrants—for example, to obtain an Andorran .ad, you must register the business name as a trademark in Andorra.

Companies that compete with the established ICANN system have created a group of non-standard suffixes. For example, New.net offers domain names with a wide range of suffixes such as .tech, .sport, .inc, .kids and .xxx. The sites using those names are not accessible by all Internet users; users must download special software to get access. Unless large Internet service providers like AOL or Microsoft agree to automatically activate these names, there's no sense investing in them.

Your domain name is more than just an address. It serves as a marketing tool and can signal to potential customers the nature of your business. Although we can't provide extensive guidance on choosing the right name—there are plenty of websites that do—we can give you one important tip. If the name is catchy and memorable, so much the better. Users are more likely to retain domain names with character and personality such as Yahoo!, ebay, Amazon and Napster.

You can register more than one domain name for your site. Multiple names can help you reach more potential customers. Naturally, if your business name is available as a domain name, you'll want to start with it. So if you own *Bernie's Bagels*, you'll very likely register berniesbagels.com as a domain name. But why stop there? Generic names can help you connect with customers who are looking for a specific product. So it would make sense to register bagels.com as well. And what about bernysbagels.com to help the bad spellers?

You and business colleagues may enjoy the creative pursuit of dreaming up a great name. Before you can use the name you come up with, however, you must register it with an approved domain name registry. (That process is explained in Section B.) Registering the name as soon as possible makes sense so you can tie up the name before someone else does.

Give A Hoot, Don't Dilute

Whatever you do, don't choose a domain name that could be confused with a famous trademark. The owner of a famous mark can stop you from using a similar name, even if there is no customer confusion. This theory (dilution) may be used against you if you're not competing in the same industry as the trademark owner. The owner of a famous trademark may claim that your domain name blurs the trademark association and weakens it. Or the claim may be that your domain name tarnishes the trademark. For example, the manufacturer of the child's game Candyland successfully sued to stop the use of candyland.com as the name of an explicit adult site.

Domain Names: How to Choose & Protect a Great Name for Your Website, by Stephen Elias and Patricia Gima (Nolo), gives extensive advice on choosing and using an effective domain name.

B. Registering a Domain Name

Before you can use a domain name, you need to register it with a domain name registry. The registration process is easy and fairly automatic—provided someone else hasn't already acquired the name you want. You just provide some minimal information to the registry and pay a modest fee, approximately $35 per name. All of this can be done online, using a credit card.

But locking up the domain name for yourself isn't enough. To avoid legal problems, you should be confident that no one else has trademark rights in the domain name before you start using it. Someone who claims such rights can invoke an arbitration procedure or take you to court to stop your use of the name.

1. Preliminary Check for Trademark Conflicts

You don't want to risk losing an inspired domain name by waiting too long. But even though speed may be important to you, at least make a cursory check for possible trademark conflicts. With a small amount of effort and no expense, you can find out whether or not there's an obvious conflict. If your desired domain name appears free of trademark conflicts, you can do a more in-depth search after you've signed up with the registry but before you go online with the name.

You can do a preliminary trademark check online in less than 15 minutes. First, look at the U.S. Patent and Trademark Office site, http://www.uspto.gov. The site contains clear instructions for conducting your search. You'll quickly find out whether anyone else owns a registered trademark identical to your domain name.

After you've visited the USPTO site, you might enter your preferred domain name in a regular search engine like http://www.google.com. The results of your search may indicate whether someone else is using the same or a very similar name for trademark or domain name purposes.

If someone else is already using the name as a trademark, you can abandon it at this early stage and save yourself the registration or reservation fee. (For more information on trademark searches, see Section D.)

> **EXAMPLE:** Jamie runs a consulting service for new businesses. She'd like to use the domain name newbiz.com but finds that it's already taken. Jamie checks at a domain name registrar to see if Protobiz is available as a domain name and fortunately, it is. She does a quick, preliminary check at the USPTO site and finds no evidence

that someone else is using protobiz (or a similar name) as a trademark. Jamie registers protobiz as a domain name so no one else can preempt her while she looks further into trademark issues.

Conflicts between a proposed domain name and an existing trademark are likely to be subtle. By now, any business with a valuable trademark has registered it as a domain name—for example, *Citibank* or *Toys 'R Us* have already been grabbed as domain names by the trademark owners. So, you're not likely to find yourself directly infringing on an existing trademark. More likely you'll face questions like whether *kittibank.com* would infringe the *Citibank* mark or *toolsareus.com* would infringe the *Toys 'R Us* mark.

There are no easy answers to issues like these, even for experienced trademark lawyers. As a small business, it's best to play it very safe. Even if there's just a small chance that a bigger company may claim infringement, it's best to back off and find another domain name. Yes, maybe you can make a convincing case that your name doesn't infringe—but you may go broke first. A bigger business will have more money, meaning it can fight longer than you can.

In the traditional brick-and-mortar world, it's often been possible for two or more separate businesses to use the same

name and have no conflict. Here are a few examples:

- Delta Airlines, Delta Dental *and* Delta Faucet
- United Airlines, United Van Lines *and* United Artists
- National Car Rental *and* National City Bank

These companies are in separate fields, so there's very little likelihood of customer confusion. But the Web is different; there can be only one united.com or one delta.com. This often causes conflict between companies that have long held legal rights to the same brand name. The legal system is just beginning to grapple with these conflicts. As a small business hoping to have a presence on the Web, your best bet is to stay out of the legal crossfire and strive for a name that seems reasonably free of possible legal conflict.

Trademarks and Service Marks

A trademark is any word, phrase, symbol or design that identifies a product brand—for example, *Compaq* computers, *Nike* shoes, *Kodak* cameras, *Xerox* photocopiers and *Marathon* gasoline. A trademark can also consist of a *combination* of words, phrases, symbols or designs.

A service mark is any word, phrase, symbol or design that identifies the provider of a service—for example, Burger King fast foods, Roto-Rooter sewer-drain service, Amazon.com retailer of books, music and other merchandise, Kinko's copy centers and Blockbuster video rentals. A service mark can also consist of a combination of words, phrases, symbols or designs. Sometimes, as in this book, the term trademark or "mark" is used to include both trademarks and service marks.

---

2. Securing Your Domain Name

To secure your domain name, register it with a domain name registry. For an alphabetical list of approved registries, go to http://www.internic.net or http://www.icann.org. Fees vary a bit among the registries, and some offer extra services such as email, website hosting, web page design or longer registration periods. (See Chapters 3 and 4 for more on designing and hosting your website.) It's also possible that your website host or developer can register your domain name for you. If someone else registers your domain name for you, be sure that you are named as the owner and as the contact person. This will assure that you receive notice of the registration.

To check on the availability of a name, go to any approved registry and look for the search feature. If the name is taken, you can learn who owns it by checking at http://www.whois.net. This is helpful in case you want to offer to buy the name. (See Section C, below, for what to do if your first choice isn't available.)

If your preferred domain name is available, you can register online using a credit card. To register the name, you'll need to provide some basic billing and business ownership information. The registry may also ask for the name of your Internet Service Provider (ISP) or the company that will be physically maintaining (hosting) your website. If you don't know this information, you can leave it blank.

Once you register your domain name, it's yours. Normally, no one can stop you from using that domain name as your Internet address. But be aware that there are some exceptions to this general rule. The primary ones are:

- **You forget to pay your domain name fees.** You need to renew your domain name and pay a fee, either yearly or every two years. If you don't, someone else can grab the name.

- **You're a cybersquatter.** You can lose the name if you registered it in bad faith—for example, with the intention of selling it to a company with a similar domain name or trademark.
- **You're infringing on someone's trademark.** If customers will be confused because your domain name is too close to another business's trademark, you may be forced to give up the name (see Section E below).
- **You're diluting someone else's famous trademark.** You're not allowed to take advantage of a very well-known trademark with an identical or similar name (see Section A sidebar, *Give a Hoot, Don't Dilute*).

⚠️ **Don't register a domain for the purpose of harming a competitor.** Be sure you have a legitimate business reason for registering a domain name. If you register a name for the primary purpose of preventing a competitor from using it as a business name, you may be violating the federal Anti-Cybersquatting Consumer Protection Act. That law makes it illegal for a person to register, traffic in or use someone else's trademark as a domain name if it's done in bad faith and with an intent to profit.

C. If Your Preferred Domain Name Is Already Taken

It's always disappointing to come up with a great domain name only to discover that someone else got there first. But take heart: All may not be lost. You have some options and strategies to consider.

1. Use a Different Suffix

If you're like many other business owners, you'll prefer to be a dot-com. But if the name you want isn't available as a .com, it may be available as a .net, .biz or .info. Keep in mind that you don't need to be a network to qualify for .net, or an information provider to use .info. Domain name registries won't quiz you about the type or form of your business.

> **EXAMPLE:** Barbi Jo has been selling women's fashion accessories under the trademark "Barbini" for 17 years. She decides to establish a website so that distributors and buyers can view her inventory. Before leaving for a trade show, Barbi Jo learns that *barbini.com* is available. But after returning, she finds that it's been acquired. She suspects a cybersquatter (someone who had talked to her at the show) but is unwilling to get involved in arbitration or a court battle. Instead, she simply registers barbini.net and establishes her website under this domain name.

2. Use a Slightly Different Name

If the exact name you want isn't available, consider using a similar one—for example, if summernight.com isn't available, maybe summersnight.com is. Make sure, however, that you're not infringing on someone else's trademark. A sound alike name is often considered an infringement—for example, smyle.com and smiles.com may both infringe the business name of smile.com. If your similar name triggers a dispute, a judge will look carefully at whether the domain names are (1) being used on commercial websites—you need to sell a product or service in order to claim trademark rights, and (2) whether your modified name is likely to confuse potential customers. In Section E, we look at the issue of customer confusion.

3. Buy the Name

If someone else owns the name you want but isn't using it, you can attempt to buy it. You can deal with the owner directly, make a bid on an auction website or use an online broker such as GreatDomains.com. A broker can help track down the owner and negotiate a good price for you.

Figuring out how much a domain name is worth is more art than science.

You can check the GreatDomains site to see how that company appraises domain names. The minimum paid for most domain names is $3,000 to $5,000. Otherwise, there are no rules for how much you should pay.

Typically, if a broker is involved, the seller will pay the broker's commission. The broker will probably provide the necessary paperwork for the transfer. If there's no broker, you can get a sample sales agreement form in *Domain Names: How to Choose & Protect a Great Name for Your Website,* by Stephen Elias and Patricia Gima (Nolo).

You may need a trademark assignment, too. If the domain name you're buying is also a registered trademark, the seller should assign all trademark rights to you. That assignment should be filed with the USPTO. For a form and further explanation, see *Trademark: Legal Care For Your Business & Product Name,* by Stephen Elias (Nolo).

After you and the seller have signed the agreement, it's up to the seller to contact the domain name registry and arrange to transfer the name to you. When you receive confirmation of the transfer, you'll pay the seller. A cautious seller may insist that a neutral third party—an escrow agent—hold your money while the transfer is taking place and then turn it over to the seller.

Rent.com?

Some domain name owners rent rather than sell domain names to others. For a fee, the company owning the name allows you to rent the name for a limited period of time, usually one year. We don't recommend this route because if you manage to build customer loyalty with your name, you'll lose that goodwill if you cannot renew the rental arrangement each year. Also, if you decide not to renew, a competing business may rent the domain name after your use and acquire your customer goodwill.

---

4. Share the Name

Businesses that offer widely different products or services have sometimes agreed to share a domain name—a far-out strategy that could work for you. One company keeps its registration, but you jointly work out an opening page that gives equal billing to both businesses. (For an example, check out http://www.northernlights.com.) Think of it as an intermediate home page. Visitors will click one link to get to your own home page or another to get to the other company's home page. From that point on you each have a separate site.

Obviously, you'll want to avoid sharing a home page with a business that may reflect poorly on yours—for example, anything pornographic. Have an attorney create a written agreement that establishes the style and content of the shared opening page—perhaps attaching a sketch of the page to the agreement. You'll also want assurances that the other company will keep the site in operation and that if the domain name owner decides to give up the name, you'd be notified in advance and will have a chance to have it transferred to you.

5. Assert Your Rights As a Senior Trademark User

If you're already in business and use a distinctive name to identify your product or service, and find that someone else is using the name online, you can, under certain circumstances, assert your rights as a "senior" trademark user. Under trademark law, the first person to use a trademark for a particular product or service owns the trademark for that class of products or services. If you used the name in commerce before the domain name registrant did, you may be able to prevent the registrant's use.

There are four routes you can use to assert your rights.

- If someone registered your trademark as a domain name, you can negotiate with the domain name owner to have the domain name assigned to you.
- If someone registered your trademark as a domain name in a bad-faith attempt to profit from it, you can use the arbitration service offered by the international organization in charge of domain name registrations (ICANN). If you win, you'll get the domain name.

- If someone registered your trademark as a domain name in bad faith, you can sue under the federal cyber-squatting law. If you win, you can get the domain name and possibly some money damages too.
- If someone is likely to confuse your customers or you have a famous mark and someone is tarnishing it, you can sue for trademark infringement. If you win, you'll get the domain name and maybe money damages as well.

Strategies for Going After Someone Using Your Trademark As a Domain Name

	ICANN Dispute Resolution Procedure	Trademark Infringement Lawsuit	Cybersquatting Lawsuit
Lawyer needed?	No	Yes	Yes
Cost	Approximately $750 to $2,500	$10,000 and up	$10,000 and up
Time	57 days from date you file your complaint	Months if the case settles, years if it goes to trial	A month or two
Who can be challenged	Any domain name registrant	As a practical matter, only U.S. registrants	As a practical matter, only U.S. registrants
What you may win	The domain name you want	The domain name you want plus money damages	The domain name you want plus money damages post-November 1999 activity

Adapted from *Domain Names: How to Choose & Protect a Great Name for Your Website*, by Stephen Elias and Patricia Gima (Nolo).

Of the four routes, we recommend ICANN arbitration for resolving domain name disputes in which the other party has taken the domain name in bad faith. It's relatively speedy and inexpensive. To see the ICANN dispute resolution rules, go to http://www.icann.org/udrp/udrp.htm. Usually an ICANN dispute is resolved within 60 days—much faster than any court decision would take. Based upon past ICANN arbitrations, the odds seem to be stacked heavily in favor of the person who has or claims to have trademark rights. If the name was not acquired in bad faith and you don't want an alternative name, your only choice is to negotiate with the domain name owner to purchase the domain name.

D. Conducting a Trademark Search

Before you start using a domain name, you should be reasonably sure that it's not going to infringe on someone else's trademark. The preliminary research we suggest doing before registering a name (Section B) should have given you a tentative green light. Now it's time for a more in-depth investigation: a trademark search. A trademark search will reveal whether your domain name is identical or very close to an existing trademark. If it is, you'll need to determine if your use of the domain name would likely confuse customers (see Section E below).

There are three main categories of trademarks to search:

- **Registered trademarks**—trademarks that have been registered with the U.S. Patent and Trademark Office (USPTO)
- **Pending registration trademarks**—names for which applications for registration have been filed with the USPTO and are pending further action, and
- **Unregistered trademarks**—trademarks that are being used in commerce but aren't pending or registered.

You can do your own trademark search on the Internet. But hiring a trademark search service to do some or all of it may give you the best legal protection for your time and money. A trademark search service will charge you about $200 to $400 per name.

1. Registered and Pending Trademarks

In Section B1, we recommended you perform a preliminary trademark search for your proposed domain name. To accomplish this, you can use the USPTO's online trademark database to compare your proposed domain name with registered and pending trademarks. You'll get a list of the trademarks that meet your search parameters, and information on how to contact the owners of those trademarks. You'll also learn how the trademark is being used (on what products or for what services) and what category of goods or services (called the "international class") the mark has been assigned to by the trademark owner or applicant. This will help you determine whether or not you can use the name without creating the likelihood of customer confusion.

If you want more information, you can perform your own high-end search on the Internet. The most comprehensive trademark searching service, called Saegis is at http://www.thomson-thomson.com. Saegis provides access to all state, federal and international trademark databases, domain name databases, common law trademarks (trademarks that are not registered with the government) and newly filed United States federal trademark applications. There's a fee for using the service.

Don't use the .com in your search. If your preferred domain name is protobiz.com, it may seem logical to search for protobiz.com in the USPTO databases. But actually, such a search would likely overlook many important marks that you should know about. It's better to focus on the protobiz part of the name. That's the part of the name that may create the likelihood of confusion.

2. Unregistered Trademarks

You won't find a list, anywhere, of unregistered trademarks, but you can use the Web to locate almost all the product and service names that may qualify as unregistered trademarks. Use any of the numerous business directories on the Web—for example, BigYellow.com, BigBook.com, SuperPages.Com, Switchboard.com or YellowPages.com—and enter your preferred domain name. A Web search engine may also yield helpful information.

3. Using a Trademark Search Service

If you'd like to be as sure as possible that your domain name won't infringe a trademark, either use Saegis (see Section D1) or pay for a search by a commercial search service. Saegis and commercial services can:

- **Furnish an up-to-date search report.** The USPTO's website is always about two to four months behind.
- **Search state (not just federal) trademark records.** Every state allows the registration of marks that are used primarily in that state. To avoid a conflict, you need to be aware of the state registrations.
- **Locate variations on and fragments of the distinctive part of your name.** Similarity in sound or appearance of just a portion of two names is sometimes enough to cause confusion. An experienced searcher can spot such problems.
- **Search proprietary databases for unregistered marks.** A search service can check out hundreds of commercial databases.

This type of advanced search is less of a necessity if you have an established brick-and-mortar business and are already familiar with the names and trademarks of your competitors. But a move on to the Web may mean that you're expanding your business into the national or international arena, in which case we recommend a commercial search. And it's always a good idea to have a search if you're starting a new business.

To initiate a commercial search, just call the search company and tell them the name you want searched. Typically, you won't see a written agreement. And the search service won't guarantee the results —in fact, it will specifically disclaim any guarantee. Three companies are commonly used for professional trademark searches:

- *Thomson & Thomson*, (http://www.thomson-thomson.com), 500 Victory Road, North Quincy, MA 02171-1545, 800-692-8833.
- *Trademark Research Corporation*, (http://www.cch-trc.com), 300 Park Avenue South, New York, NY 10010, 800-TRC-MARK.
- *Sunnyvale Center on Innovation, Invention and Ideas* (Sc[i]³) pronounced Sigh-Cubed (http://www.sci3.com), 465 South Mathilda Avenue, Suite 300, Sunnyvale, CA 94086 408-730-7290.

This last company—Sc[i]³—is especially attractive because it's affiliated with the USPTO and charges less than most other searching companies. As of October 2001, Sc[i]³ charged $199 for a complete online analytical search (including state and federal trademark registers and common law sources). As with most trademark search firms, Sc[i]³ doesn't interpret its results; it leaves that to you.

4. Evaluating Your Search Results

A trademark search, whether you perform it yourself or hire a service to do it for you, is rarely conclusive. If you turn up trademarks that might conflict with yours, you need to decide if using your proposed domain name would be likely to cause customer confusion. (See Section E.) For additional peace of mind, you may want to review the results of your trademark search with a lawyer who is an expert on trademarks. If you conclude that your domain name won't infringe on someone else's trademark, then you can also consider registering the domain name with the USPTO as a trademark. (See Section F.) Keep in mind that registering a domain name with a domain name registry is a separate and much different process than registering a name as a trademark.

E. Evaluating the Likelihood of Customer Confusion

As a general rule, if you think your name may infringe another business's trademark, we advise you to take a cautious approach and pick something different. That's the easiest way to avoid any potential legal entanglements. But if you'd like a little more guidance about whether to keep or ditch a domain name, the key issue to consider is whether your use of your domain name will create a likelihood of customer confusion.

Example: Yahoo! Inc. has trademarked the word *yahoo*. Eitan—a man who has no association with Yahoo! Inc.—registers several domain names with a domain name registry, including: *jahu, wyahoo, youhoo* and *yuahoo*. Yahoo! Inc. files a complaint against Eitan under ICANN's dispute resolution procedure. The panelist assigned to the complaint determines that Eitan's names are confusingly similar to the trademarked name *yahoo* and that Eitan registered the names so he could trade on the goodwill and fame associated with the *yahoo* mark. The names that Eitan registered are transferred to Yahoo! Inc.

Example: Advance Magazine Publishers Inc. publishes *Vogue,* a well-known fashion magazine. The company has registered several names as trademarks, including *Vogue* and *Teen Vogue* and has also registered *vogue.com* as a domain name. When Advance Magazine Publishers tries to register *teenvogue.com* as a domain name, it discovers that Frank and his company, Vogue International, have already registered that domain name for a website that sells cosmetics and clothes. Advance Magazine Publishers sues Frank and his company in federal court, alleging trademark infringement. The judge finds that the *teenvogue.com* domain name is confusingly similar to the *Vogue* trademark. Since there is a high likelihood that Advance Magazine Publishers will win its lawsuit, the judge issues a preliminary injunction, ordering Frank to stop using *teenvogue.com.*

In deciding infringement claims, courts ask: Is it more likely than not that a reasonable customer would be confused by the simultaneous use of the same or similar names? Absolute certainty isn't required. The business that's challenging a name only has to show that confusion is *probable*—not that it actually has occurred.

Most of the time, confusion means that the goods or services a customer buys are different than what the customer intended to buy. For instance, suppose your aunt recommends that you buy some GramJam preserves that are prepared by her friend Joyce and sold only on the Web. You decide to order two jars of peach preserves, but instead of typing gramjam.com into your browser, you type grandjam.com instead. GrandJam is a competing business run by Louise; she copied GramJam's idea of selling preserves on the Web, with only a minor variation in the name. You order the preserves without knowing that you ordered the wrong product from the wrong website.

The other kind of customer confusion occurs when a misleading name causes customers to believe—wrongly—that a product or service is sponsored by, approved of or is somehow connected with a business they already know about. In other words, customers are confused about the source of the product or service. This would be the case, for example, if you took your printer to a repair shop called Dell Service Company because you thought that Dell, the computer company, somehow sponsored the business.

Below are some basic principles that will help you assess customer confusion.

For more information on customer confusion issues, consult *Trademark: Legal Care for Your Business & Product Name,* by Stephen Elias (Nolo).

- If your goods or services are closely related, the risk of customer confusion is high. If your goods or services are unrelated to those of the trademark owner, you may have a solid right to use a trademarked word in your domain name.

- If the goods and services you offer on your website compete directly with those identified by a competing mark, a court would probably find a likelihood of customer confusion if your domain name is similar in sound, appearance or meaning.

- The closer the names are in sound or appearance, the more likely it is that you'll have a problem.

- The weaker a trademark—that is, the less it distinguishes goods or services— the more difficult it is to protect.

- The more expensive an item is, the less chance that a similar name will cause customer confusion.
- If your business sells to the same customers as the other business, there's a greater chance for customer confusion.
- If the potentially conflicting name is being used for a number of products and services marketed by another business—even if your product or service is unrelated to them—you're more likely to have a problem.

An experienced trademark lawyer can help you assess the risks. A lawyer who's familiar with the many court decisions in trademark infringement cases should have an informed opinion on whether you're likely to be sued or taken before a domain name panel, and, if so, what the outcome will be.

F. Registering Your Domain Name As a Trademark

You're the owner of a trademark if you're the first to use it. That principle also applies to a domain name that functions as your trademark. Whether or not you've registered the name with the U.S. Patent and Trademark Office, you can stop someone else's subsequent use of a similar mark on similar goods and service.

Registering your trademark with the PTO gives you additional benefits. For one thing, it makes it easier for you to enforce your rights as a trademark owner. You'll be *presumed* to own the mark, and anyone who later uses it is presumed to know about it. This makes it a bit easier to convince a judge that the later user is intentionally infringing on your mark. If you are able to prove the infringement was intentional, it can put more money in your pocket. The possibility of suing for enhanced damages will make it easier to find a lawyer to take your case if someone infringes on your trademark.

If you registered a business name as a trademark before you made it part of your domain name, you needn't register the domain name separately. For example, let's say you've been selling socks under the name Hotsocks and you've registered that name as a trademark with the USPTO. Now you decide to sell socks online and you name your website hotsocks.com. There's no need to register hotsocks.com as a trademark— though you might consider doing so if you were offering some unique service online apart from the socks.

Not all names can be registered as trademarks. For example, you will have a challenge registering a generic name like drugs.com as a trademark. And you'd face an uphill struggle to register a domain name that you use solely as an address and not a signifier of services. For example, the law firm of Smith & Jones would have a hard time registering smith&jones.com as a trademark. It would have to prove that the domain name is being used for some other purpose than for people to find and contact the law firm. For more information, review the USPTO publication, "Trademark Examination of Domain Names," available at http://www.uspto.gov/web/offices/tac/notices/guide299.htm.

Once you decide you have a name you can register as a trademark, it's a breeze to file your trademark application online at the USPTO website (http://www.uspto.gov). The typical filing fee for a domain name mark is $325 per class (kind of goods or services). It can be more, however, if you'll be offering a number of different services on your website. To complete the registration process, you have to actually be using the domain name on a website. But you can start the process if you intend to use the name soon, by using something called an intent-to-use application. When you do start using the name and complete the registration process, the application date will be treated as the date you first used the mark. This will give you a priority claim over later users. When you file an intent-to-use application and then complete the process after you begin using the domain name, you pay an additional $100 fee.

The USPTO may take a year or more to process your application but once you file it, your domain name will appear as a pending trademark in the USPTO database. If you file a "use" application (one based on your actual use of the name), you'll probably hear from the USPTO in three to six months. If there's a problem, you'll get a letter explaining it. In many cases, you'll be able to solve the problem with a phone call. At some point, you should receive a Notice of Publication. The USPTO will then publish your mark in its *Official Gazette,* allowing people to oppose your registration. Assuming there is no opposition, you'll receive a Certificate of Registration or, in the case of an intent-to-use mark that has not been placed in commerce, a Notice of Allowance.

Later on, there will be some housekeeping chores to keep your registration in force. For example, between five and six years after registering your mark, you'll need to inform the USPTO that you're still using it. You must renew your registration every ten years. ■

Creating Your Website

Developing the best website you can is a challenging and important part of taking your business online. Your site must have a pleasing, functional design, and it must accurately reflect your business's persona. If it doesn't, you'll lose customers and good will.

Creating an effective e-commerce website is not rocket science, but it's not child's play either. If you're technologically gifted and have some design experience, you may be able to pull it off without outside help. But no one can legitimately accuse you of being a computer wimp if you decide that developing a website isn't a do-it-yourself project. Like many businesses, you may prefer to let a professional website developer put your site together. This chapter can help you decide whether to prepare your own site or hire a developer. And, if you do hire a developer, we provide a sample development agreement and explain the development process.

A. Visualize Your Site

Whether you create the website yourself or use a developer, you must have some notion of what you'd like your site to do and what it should look like. Early in the game, you should have answers for the following questions:

- Will you use the site mainly to provide information for your products and services?
- Will the site tell people where they can go to see or buy your products?
- Will you encourage people to communicate with you by email or by phone?
- Will you take orders online?
- If so, how do you plan to process payments, and how do you envision the checkout process?
- Will your site provide links to other sites and, if so, which ones?

If you've had a brick-and-mortar business for several years, you may have a head start on figuring out how your site should look, especially if you have a preferred style for your brochures, catalogs and other promotional literature. You can adapt these stylistic preferences, as well as any logos or other company graphics, to the website medium. That will provide continuity and uniformity.

But even if you don't have prepared materials to work with, you can still come up with good ideas. The easiest way to get design ideas is to visit a number of other sites. Print out some pages that look good to you and that function the way you'd like your own site to function.

Mark these pages with your comments such as: "Good organization," "Typeface looks great," "I like the way the pages are linked" or "Good model for an About Our Company page." Equally helpful is to look at sites and decide what you *don't* want. Again, print out Web pages and mark features that are inappropriate—for example, "Animation on home page too distracting."

It's a mistake to believe that the best sites are the ones with the most razzle-dazzle. If you have too many bells and whistles, you'll wind up with a slow, klutzy, confusing site. Here are some basic principles to think about as you begin to create your site.

Make sure your home page loads quickly. The average Internet surfer uses a 56K telephone modem. One rule to follow is that every page at your site should download within seven seconds on a 56K modem. Customers won't sit patiently while your home page slowly comes to life on their computer monitor. They'll click to another site. Bottom line: Be prepared to dump some fancy features to cut down on the load time.

Don't let your important messages get lost in clutter. Often, as the saying goes, less is more. Figure out what you want to say. Then make sure it comes through loud and clear on the user's computer screen.

Remember that not everyone owns a huge monitor. See that your important information fits comfortably and legibly on a 15" computer screen. And recognize that some users don't like to scroll a page to get to information. You may be better

off to whisk users to another page if the additional information is important.

Skip the fancy stuff. Until users everywhere have the right computer tools for music and animation, stick to the basics that are within the reach of virtually every surfer. Gimmicks slow down your site and distract from your core message anyway.

Don't try to do it all on your home page. You probably need different pages for different purposes: advertising your products and services, telling people about your business, taking orders, soliciting email or seeking new employees.

Answer common questions. The Web is rich with free information, and customers have come to expect it. Keep track of the questions people ask about your products and services and answer them using the FAQ (Frequently Asked Questions) format. You can also link customers to other sites that offer valuable information that your customers likely will be interested in. The Web is all about linking, so take full advantage of that feature.

Colleagues and employees may be helpful in coming up with suggestions about the look and feel of the site. In a truly small business—one with fewer than ten employees—that could include everyone in the company. Let all employees know you're thinking of having an e-commerce website. Encourage them to come up with ideas about what it should be like. Then hold a brainstorming session in which all ideas can be presented and discussed. A side benefit is that working together on a project like this can boost company morale.

For insights into how people really use websites, and how to design one for maximum effectiveness, check out www.useit.com, the site of usability guru Jakob Neilsen.

B. Can You Do It Yourself?

If you're like the businesses profiled in Chapter 1, the odds are that you'll be much better off letting someone else design your website for you. But creating your site by yourself has some advantage: you save money, and you have the knowledge and skills to maintain your site and make changes without the aid of an outside contractor. To create your own website, you'll need to fit the following profile:

- **You're technically savvy.** You have to be fearless when it comes to learning new programs—for example, Microsoft *Front Page* or Macromedia *Dreamweaver*—and you must be comfortable with computer terminology and technology. Unless you're quite talented behind the mouse, it will take you several weeks to master the features of most website design programs. And without a doubt, you'll make at least a few mistakes before you get it right.

- **You have a have a flair for design and graphics.** You must know how to lay out graphics and text in a professional manner and have an eye for choosing the right photos and art. Even if you have a design flair, it often helps to bring in a third party to enhance your vision. Remember, just because *you* like the way your site looks doesn't mean it will impress your customers.

- **You understand how people use websites.** People read books and watch TV, but they use websites to find what they want as quickly as they can. You need to know something about usability before you can design a website that functions the way it should.

- **You have plenty of time.** Website design is remarkably time-consuming. It can be enjoyable and satisfying, but chances are that if you're like most people creating a site, you'll find yourself staring bleary-eyed at a monitor at 3 a.m. Your time is money. Could you spend your time more wisely and efficiently doing what you know how to do, which is run your business?

Even if you meet these do-it-yourself qualifications, you may be limited to creating a rudimentary or passive website. The addition of shopping carts and internal search features may still be beyond your grasp. If you are interested in incorporating storefront functionality such as shopping carts, there are storefront development kits available online. For example, check Miva at http://www.miva.com.

If you do create your own site, we strongly advise you to test it ("beta testing" is the tech term) by posting it for friends and associates to view and use before you make it available to the public. You can usually do this for free. The Internet Service Provider (ISP) with whom you maintain an email account probably offers free space for your website material. You'll have a special, temporary online address for friends and associates to use when checking out your site. Later, when you're satisfied with your website and it's time to go public with it, you'll need to pay for a hosting service; this will let everyone get to your site by using your domain name. (For information on hosting services, see Chapter 4.)

Beta testing allows you to get feedback and to test the site's functionality—for example, whether or not the links work and pictures appear. You can also get opinions on the site's usability—whether it confuses visitors or helps them. Only after you're satisfied with all of the site's elements should you transfer it to a hosting service and use your domain name.

C. Getting Help Creating a Website: Your Options

If you decide not to create your site yourself, you have three alternatives when it comes to getting professional help:

Buy a package deal. You can sign up for a package deal with an Internet Service Provider (ISP) such as AOL, a Web portal such as Yahoo! or an Internet domain name registrar such as Verisign, which will provide website design services and host your website for free or for a token charge. Going the package route is a low-cost way to get up and running on the Web. This type of site is usable and works reasonably well, although some ISP sponsored sites have a canned look that is indistinguishable from that of thousands of other websites. Another concern may be whether you receive enough storage space on the company's computers to house a truly classy website.

The procedure for creating one of these built-on-demand sites is straightforward: you choose a template (a basic structure or organization for your site), select a color scheme, pick graphics, answer questions about your business and enter descriptive text when appropriate, choose shopping cart options and the ISP or hosting service (see below) takes care of the rest. *Voila!* You have an instant store. To learn more about these types of websites and to see examples, check out Earthlink at http:///www.earthlink.net/biz, Yahoo Shopping at http://shopping. yahoo.com (click on "Yahoo!Store") or Web Business by Verisign at http:// www.verisign.com.

Buy development services from a Web host. Some Web hosting services (discussed in Chapter 4) offer website development services as well. Usually you pay for these services separately from the hosting services, although some hosting services combine the services. Depending on the experience and competence of the host's development team or website creation software, this can be a worthwhile option. To see examples of these types of services, check out Homestead (http:// www.homestead.com) or ZyWeb (http:// www.zyweb.com).

These first two alternatives—buying a package deal from an ISP or web host— are the easiest ways to get up and running. They may be ideal if you want to try out selling products on the Web before committing to the expense of developing a custom website.

Hire an independent website developer. The third—and probably the best—

option for most small businesses is to hire an independent developer (someone not tied directly to an ISP or Web hosting company) developer to create a custom site for you. If you go this route, you'll have greater control over the final product and will be more likely to be pleased with the result. Typically, you'll be working with an individual or a small firm that will be tuned in to the needs of small businesses such as yours. The remainder of this chapter is devoted to hiring an independent website developer.

D. Choosing a Website Developer

Hiring a website developer, like hiring any independent contractor, requires researching the candidates and negotiating a proposal to get the job done. In the following sections, we'll guide you through the process.

1. Finding an Independent Website Developer

As with hiring any professional, it's a good idea to put together a short list of prospects. Usually you'll do best with referrals from owners of other small businesses who have taken the plunge into e-commerce. You can also turn to obvious sources such as the Yellow Pages or the Web itself. (Typing "website developer" into a search engine will unleash hundreds of prospects.)

It's easy to see examples of a developer's work. Simply type the developer's name into a search engine to view sites created by the developer. Even better, in some cases, is to do it backwards: surf the Web until you find several sites that are appealing and look like something you'd like for yourself. Then, find out who created the site (sometimes there's an online credit), and make a call or send an email to learn more.

Since working with a website developer is a creative partnership, get as much information as you can about how easy or hard it is to work with the people or firms you're considering—and whether they meet their deadlines. To get the inside scoop, you'll need to speak to other business owners for whom the developer has created sites. This should also be easy; simply click the "contact us" or "email" links on those business websites.

Finally, keep in mind that some face-to-face communication can be helpful in any business deal. If you're in or near a major metropolitan area, chances are you'll be able to find several small and highly qualified website development firms to talk to. At least it's worth a try. Personal chemistry does play a definite role in the process. Some developers may talk to you for an hour or two at no charge just to get a feel for the project.

Don't be rigid in dealing with the developer. Working with a developer is like working with an architect who will design a house for you or a landscaper who will install a flower garden. You need to provide as much insight as you can into what you're looking for. Even though you're the ultimate arbiter of what the site should look like and do, keep an open mind when the website developer makes suggestions. After all, the developer is (presumably) a pro who can offer helpful ideas in addition to technical expertise.

2. Your Request for Proposal

A request for proposal (RFP) is an invitation to website developers to tell you what they can do to meet your needs and how much they'd charge. Presenting your ideas in an RFP will give website developers something concrete to work with. Later, if you've given enough details, the RFP can be used as the basis for writing a contract. Your RFP should include a bit of information about your business, the look and feel you're trying to achieve for your website and your ideas about how users will interact with the site. Below is an example.

Request for Proposal

ProtoBiz is a design company that specializes in the creation of mechanical and digital prototypes. We're interested in creating a website that showcases our services and provides a method for potential clients to securely submit information. We would also like to operate a purchasing/shopping cart service to sell accessories that feature our logo such as t-shirts, cups and aprons. The purpose of this letter is to solicit a proposal from your firm to create our website.

Our Requirements. The following are the specific requirements for our site, which we may amend later:

- In addition to a home page, we will need four sections (with subsections) that should total approximately 40 Web pages. These sections include: About Us (the company's history and work environment), Our Clients (information about our clientele), ProtoBiz Projects (examples of our work for clients) and Becoming a Client of Protobiz (a description of our work methods and how prospective clients can submit requests for bids on prototype work).
- We do not want opening screen animation.
- We would like a system for a user to search the website.
- We need a shopping cart and secure online order processing system with the ability to take credit card payments for our sales of accessories.
- We would like to make it possible to provide secure uploads of client submissions.
- We would like to launch the site by May 15, 20XX.
- We require ownership of the website design and appearance but not of the underlying technology or authoring tools.

Please provide us with your estimate of the cost for the project as well as information about your company, including a client list. If possible, please describe how you go about creating websites. We would be happy to speak with you by phone or in person if that would help you understand our needs better.

Sincerely,

PROTOBIZ

Claudia Pandora

President

It's best to talk to a developer before sending an RFP. You can, if you wish, send your RFP to several developers at once and compare the estimates.

E. The Website Development Agreement

If you're having someone perform website development, get the agreement in writing. There are too many legal issues involved to leave it to a handshake. Chances are that the developer will provide you with a proposed written contract. In that case, you can use our sample agreement, below, and the accompanying explanations to evaluate the developer's agreement.

The smaller the website design firm, the more flexibility you'll have in contract negotiations. Larger firms often have standard contracts and may be willing to discuss and make only minor changes. Not so with a smaller firm. Here, you're likely to have much more to say about the shape of the deal. The smaller firm may not even have a contract to use as a starting point.

1. What a Website Development Agreement Should Contain

Whether you use our Website Development Agreement or the developer's, your agreement should deal with the following issues:

- **Specifications and timelines.** You'll need to reach agreement with the developer on the details of the website and when work should be completed.
- **Warranties and indemnity.** You'll need assurances from the developer that the work will not create legal problems such as claims of copyright infringement or libel.
- **Who owns the work.** You'll need to be able to claim copyright ownership of the site's design and appearance.
- **Assigning the contract.** If you don't want the developer assigning the work to someone else, you'll need to prevent assignment of the agreement.
- **Objections and approvals.** You'll want a simple system for approving or objecting to the developer's work.
- **Termination.** You'll want an escape hatch in case things turn sour during the development process.

The agreement below deals with the issues discussed above and more. Explanations of each provision are provided after each section of the agreement. For additional information, see Customizing Written Contracts at the end of this chapter.

The agreement in this chapter may be found on the CD-ROM at the back of the book.

2. A Sample Website Development Agreement

Website Development Agreement

1. Names

This Agreement is made by _____ (Developer) and
_____ (Client).

Explanation: *For information on how to enter each party's name properly, see Customizing Written Contracts at the end of this chapter.*

2. Definitions

The Site means a series of linked Web pages under common control and developed by Developer for Client under this Agreement.

Client Content means all data, code, trademarks and copyrighted content provided by Client for use by Developer on the Site.

Developer Content means all data, code, trade secrets, patents, designs, drawings and text created by Developer for use on the Site, including any modifications or enhancements provided by Developer. Developer Content does not mean software development or authoring tools or similar material created by Developer or licensed from third parties for use in creating websites.

Explanation: *Clause 8 of the agreement says you own the copyright to Developer Content; these definitions help to establish what that gives you. We've excluded certain technology and authoring tools from the definition of developer content. That's because developers often use these tools on many sites, and it's unusual for a small business to acquire ownership.*

If you operate a small Web business, it's unlikely that you will need to acquire ownership of Web-authoring tools. Keep in mind, however, that some online companies have demanded and acquired ownership of developer-created authoring tools. This has happened when those tools were crucial to the online business and when the business wanted to be sure that other sites couldn't use them—for example, the developer created a unique method of reviewing purchases before completing a transaction.

3. Developer Services

Developer will perform the services described in Attachment 1. There are four stages of development services: Concept, Design, Initial Development and Final Development. Developer will complete the four stages on or before the dates listed in Attachment 1. Before delivering the Site to Client, Developer will test its components to make sure the Site and its components work as intended.

Explanation: *We've divided the development process into four stages to break the project into bite-sized pieces and allow you to change course at various checkpoints. You can dump the developer and start over with someone else if things aren't going well.*

In the concept stage, you and the developer simply work on specifications and concepts. This is a good way to check on whether your ideas for the site are workable. It also lets you try out the working relationship with the developer. After that, the design stage should allow you to have a good idea of what the site will be. That's followed by the initial and final development stages.

4. Compensation

As Developer completes each stage, Client will pay Developer the fees stated in Attachment 1.

Explanation:*Typically, you and the website developer will agree on a cash price for the work. That doesn't mean, however, that you'll pay it in a lump sum. More likely, your deal will be that you'll pay in installments as the developer achieves certain milestones set out in Attachment 1. And you always want a chance to review content or test the operation of the website before you make an installment payment. It's a good idea to agree that at the end of the job you can hold back some part of the final payment until you've made sure the website works as promised. The hold-back period can last for several weeks or even months, depending on how the contract is written. You can customize Attachment 1 to provide for such a holdback.*

If your business is strapped for cash and the developer is willing to be flexible, you may be able to negotiate non-cash compensation. For example, a developer might be willing to create your website and to receive, as payment, a portion of the money you take in from the site.

EXAMPLE: *Suzi writes a monthly newsletter for pet owners. She feels she can boost subscriptions by marketing the newsletter online to new subscribers who would receive each edition by email. Because Suzi has been in business for only six months and doesn't know yet if her venture will become profitable, she's reluctant to contract with a website developer for a fixed fee. After talking to several developers who want a traditional cash arrangement, she meets Mike, who's willing to consider other options. Although it is a risk for Mike, he agrees that his payment will depend on the success of the site. Suzi will pay Mike 25% of the first year's revenue she receives from new online subscribers.*

5. **Evaluation and Acceptance**

As Developer completes each stage, Developer will submit the completed materials to Client for approval. Client will have _____ days to approve the completed materials or provide corrections and comments. If Client fails to provide approval or comments during any of the approval periods, those materials will be considered to be approved.

Developer will have _____ days after receiving Client's comments and corrections to submit a revised version of the materials to Client. Client will review the revised version within _____ days of receipt and either approve the corrected version or make further changes.

If Client determines, in its reasonable discretion, that the materials are not acceptable after two attempts at correction by Developer, Client may terminate this Agreement.

Explanation: *Once the project is underway, you need a chance at various points to review what's been done and to accept or reject it. In addition to reviewing the specifications, for example, you need to look at each page of the site before it's final to make sure you're satisfied with the content and look. An important principle to capture in your contract is that nothing is final until you approve it. If something isn't acceptable to you, the developer must go back to the virtual drawing board and revise it until it's right.*

6. **Delays and Progress Reports**

Developer will send weekly progress reports to Client describing the status of development. If Developer anticipates that it will not complete an assignment according to the timetable in Attachment 1, Developer will promptly notify Client in writing and will propose a new timetable. Unless Client and Developer agree on a new timetable, Developer will proceed under the previously agreed-upon schedule.

Explanation: *This provision guarantees that you're kept informed, weekly, of the status of the work.*

7. **Work for Competitors**

While working for Client, Developer will not work for any other person or company engaged in the _____ business.

Explanation: *Obviously, you don't want the developer working on a competitor's site while working on yours.*

8. **Assignment of Rights**

Developer assigns to Client all rights, title and interest in the copyrights in Developer Content, including copyright in the Site's compilation or collective work and in the derivative copyrights of such works. Developer will sign any further documents reasonably requested by Client to put into effect the assignment of these rights. Developer retains a royalty-free license to use, copy, modify, display, distribute and sublicense the underlying software and authoring code for other clients.

Explanation: *It's essential that you deal with content ownership issues in your contract. If you don't you may only obtain a limited right to post the site and the developer will own the copyright. You may not even have the right to make copies of the site or modify its components. This clause gives you maximum ownership rights. The developer may be reluctant to give up all rights to some of the technical features or tools developed for the site. That's a reasonable position since the developer may want to use some of these tools in constructing other people's sites. If the developer wants to retain ownership and be able to use this stuff on future jobs, delete the last sentence and substitute the following: "Developer retains ownership of any authoring code or similar development tools created by Developer and grants to Client an unlimited nonexclusive license to use such tools solely in conjunction with the Site."*

9. Website Credits and Links

Developer may:

❏ state on the Site that Developer developed the Site

❏ place hypertext links on the Site to Developer's website.

Client must approve in advance the size and placement of such notices and links on the Site in advance.

Explanation: *Most developers insist on some form of credit. You might, however, get a price break for providing it, since this exposure could lead to more jobs for the developer. You can even offer to provide a link from your site to the developer's own site. None of this costs you anything or affects the operation of your site. Our form includes two optional rights you can grant the developer. Simply check the boxes for the ones that you agree on.*

10. Client Warranties

Client warrants to Developer that Client has the authority to enter into this Agreement and has or will obtain all necessary and appropriate rights and licenses to grant the license to Developer to use Client Content for the Site.

Explanation: *Here, you assure the developer that you have the legal authority to sign the agreement. You also promise that you'll get any licenses you need for the content you supply.*

11. Indemnification by Client

Client will indemnify Developer from any third-party claims resulting in losses, damages, liabilities, costs, charges and expenses, including reasonable attorney fees, arising out of any breach of any of Client's warranties contained in this Agreement. For such indemnification to be effective, however, Developer must give Client prompt written notice of any such claim and provide Client such reasonable cooperation and assistance as Client may request in the defense of the suit. Client will have sole control over any such suit or proceeding.

Explanation: *This clause says that if someone sues the developer because you didn't get permission to use the content you're supplying, you'll pay the developer's legal expenses—and any damages that are awarded against the developer. If you have the permission you should have, it won't cause you any headaches.*

12. Developer Representations and Warranties

Developer warrants to Client that:
- The Site will meet all specifications set forth in this Agreement and its attachments.
- The Site will operate as intended and will be developed in accordance with all applicable laws, rules and regulations.
- Developer has obtained or will obtain all necessary and appropriate rights and licenses to use Developer Content for the Site.
- Developer will provide Client with copies of clearances obtained from third parties for the use on the Site of any copyrighted, trademarked or other legally protected material.
- The Site (excluding Client Content) will not infringe the rights of any third parties.
- Developer will not engage in any defamatory, deceptive, misleading or unethical practices that are or might be detrimental to Client or the Site.

Explanation: *It's wise to have the developer make a number of statements and promises that you can rely on later if things go wrong and the developer runs for cover. For example, after your site begins operating, you may learn that the developer failed to get permission to use copyrighted material owned by a third party. The clause in our contract gives you a legal basis for suing the developer, if that becomes necessary—but will help you only if the developer has deep pockets. Promises from a financially strapped developer are, for all practical purposes, worthless.*

Still, asking for them can't hurt and may help. They should cover both the operation and content of the website. On the operation side, have the developer warrant that the site will meet all your specifications and that it will operate as intended. If it doesn't, then the developer should be responsible for fixing it or paying the cost of getting it fixed. Most developers will be willing to guarantee their work—but not forever. Obviously, a one-year warranty is better than a 90-day or six-month warranty. Get the longest warranty you can negotiate.

On the content side, you'd like a warranty that the developer has gotten the permission needed for you to use all content on the site—for example, if the developer is using stock photos or clip art. Of course, no such warranty is needed for the content you've created yourself. The developer should also warrant that the content won't violate anyone's rights and that it contains nothing defamatory.

13. **Indemnification by Developer**

Developer will indemnify Client from any third-party claims resulting in losses, damages, liabilities, costs, charges and expenses, including reasonable attorney fees, arising out of any breach of any of Developer's warranties contained in this Agreement. For such indemnification to be effective, however, Client must give Developer prompt written notice of any such claim and provide Developer such reasonable cooperation and assistance as Developer may request in the defense of such suit. Developer will have sole control over any such suit or proceeding.

If a claim of infringement is made regarding an element of the Site, Developer will promptly, and at its own expense, replace that element with a similar but non-infringing element.

Explanation: *Our contract requires the developer to indemnify you if you're sued because the developer messed up. For example, this clause requires the developer to pay your legal expenses if you're sued and any damages awarded against you. Be aware, though, that the indemnity requirement is only as good as the developer's financial resources. If you're hit with a $50,000 verdict for copyright infringement and the developer has only $2,000 in the bank, the indemnity clause won't help you much. So have the developer identify the source of each piece of content and what permission has been granted. Keep a file of permission letters from copyright owners.*

14. **Developer Disclaimer**

Developer does not warrant the performance of the Site to the extent such performance is not under the control of Developer or Developer's Web Host.

Explanation: *This clause says the developer won't be responsible for site performance problems that it can't control—for example, a computer virus that compromises the site's performance.*

15. Confidentiality

The parties acknowledge that each owns valuable trade secrets (Confidential Information) and that each party will have access to the other party's Confidential Information in carrying out this Agreement. Each party will:

- Hold and maintain the other party's Confidential Information in strict confidence and in trust for the sole benefit of the other party.
- Restrict access to the other party's Confidential Information to persons bound by this Agreement.
- Obtain the prior written approval of the other party before using the other party's Confidential Information for its own benefit, or publishing or otherwise disclosing it to others, or permitting others to use it for their benefit or to the detriment of the other party.
- Take all necessary action to protect the confidentiality of the other party's Confidential Information.
- Indemnify the other party against any and all losses, damages, claims or expenses incurred or suffered by the other party as a result of any breach of this Section 15.

The parties' obligations under this Section do not extend to information that is:

- generally known to the public
- discovered or created by either party independent of any involvement with the other party or the Confidential Information, or
- learned by either party through legitimate means other than from the other party or anyone connected with the other party.

Explanation: *In working on your site, the developer will probably have access to some sensitive information about your business—material you wouldn't want competitors to know about. This clause requires the developer to maintain this information in confidence, and not share it with others or use it on other jobs.*

Chances are that even without such a clause, a responsible developer would be well aware of the need to safeguard your business data and plans. Still, it can't hurt to drive home the message with a specific commitment in the contract.

Note that the clause is reciprocal. You'll have to protect the secrecy of the developer's confidential information that comes your way.

16. Survival

The provisions of Sections 10 through 15 will survive any termination of this Agreement.

Explanation: *Sections 10 through 15 will stay in effect even after the job is done or the contract is ended.*

17. Term of Agreement

This Agreement takes effect on _____ and will continue in effect until the completion of the four stages listed in Attachment 1 unless terminated earlier according to this Agreement.

Explanation: *Here, insert the starting date of the agreement. It may be the day you both sign it or some other date. Unless you or the developer terminate it, the agreement stays in effect until the job is done. As pointed out above, some parts of the contract stay in effect even after the contract ends.*

18. Termination Due to Breach

Either party may terminate this Agreement at any time if the other party breaches or fails to observe any of its obligations under this Agreement and such breach or failure is not cured within 30 days after the non-breaching party notifies the other party in writing of the breach or failure.

Explanation: *Either you or the developer can terminate the agreement if the other party has violated its terms. But before terminating the deal for a violation (sometimes called a breach of contract), you or the developer must give a 30-day notice so the other party can try to repair (cure) the breach.*

19. Client's Right to Terminate

Client may terminate this contract:

❏ If, after two attempts at correction, Client fails to approve Developer's completion of a stage of development; or

❏ If Developer fails to revise and resubmit work rejected by Client within the time required by this contract; or

❏ At Client's sole discretion and upon _____ days written notice to Developer.

In the event of termination for any of the reasons set forth in this section, Developer will be entitled to (a) all fees for work previously approved as set forth in Attachment A and (b) for payment of all unapproved work at Developer's hourly rate of _____.

Explanation: *You can end the contract if the developer, after two tries, doesn't fix a problem to your satisfaction, or the developer doesn't meet the contract deadlines for revising and resubmitting rejected work. You can also end after simply giving the developer written notice*

that you'll be doing so. You'll need to insert a time period in the contract—perhaps ten days. If you terminate the contract for any of the reasons in this section, the developer is entitled to payment for all work performed prior to cancellation. That would include all fees due for approved work and payment for work that had been performed, but not approved. You and developer should agree on and insert an hourly rate to use in this section. Website development rates are between $30–$100 an hour.

20. Rights Upon Termination

If either party terminates this contract:

Client will have no further obligation to Developer except to pay for work as set forth in this Agreement and in accordance with the compensation schedule in Attachment 1. Developer will promptly deliver to Client all work performed and accepted as of the time of termination and return all materials supplied by Client.

Explanation: *If either of you ends the contract, you must pay for work; the developer must deliver that work to you, along with material you've supplied.*

21. Designated Representatives

Each party will designate a representative to receive and send materials, approvals, comments, invoices and other materials discussed in this agreement.

Developer's Representative will be:

Name: _____

Address: _____

_____

Phone: _____

Fax: _____

Email: _____

Client's Representative will be:

Name: _____

Address: _____

_____

Phone: _____

Fax: _____

Email: _____

Explanation: *Insert the name and contact information for each party's designated representative.*

22. Website Maintenance and New Development

Developer will maintain the Site or provide additional development after its launch according to the terms stated in Attachment 2.

Explanation: *If you're not tech-savvy or you don't have the time or inclination to do it yourself, you'll need a person or firm on tap to keep your site running properly and to assist in keeping it up to date. For example, you may want to add material or features from time to time, or change or delete some of the content. The developer may be willing to take on these ongoing chores. If so, you can include the arrangements in your development contract —or perhaps sign a second, separate contract.*

The argument for having it all in one contract is that you'll have continuity, since the developer will know all about the site. But there's also a benefit to having a separate contract: you can wait and see how your relationship with the developer works out before signing on for a long-term commitment.

We provide this optional contract clause here for you to consider.

23. Disputes

(Choose One)

❐ Mediation. If a dispute arises, the parties will try in good faith to settle it through mediation conducted by:

_____

❐ a mediator to be mutually selected.

The parties will share the costs of the mediator equally. Each party will cooperate fully and fairly with the mediator and will attempt to reach a mutually satisfactory resolution to the dispute. If the dispute is not resolved within 30 days after it is referred to the mediator, either party may take the matter to court.

❐ Mediation and Possible Arbitration. If a dispute arises, the parties will try in good faith to settle it through mediation conducted by:

_____

❐ a mediator to be mutually selected.

The parties will share the costs of the mediator equally. Each party will cooperate fully and fairly with the mediator and will attempt to reach a mutually satisfactory solution to the dispute. If the dispute is not resolved within 30 days after it is referred to the mediator, it will be arbitrated by:

_____

❐   an arbitrator to be mutually selected.

Judgment on the arbitration award may be entered in any court that has jurisdiction over the matter. The arbitrator will allocate costs of arbitration, including attorney fees.

Explanation: _See Customizing Written Contracts at the end of this chapter. This clause is optional. If you don't use it, either party can sue over any dispute._

24. Relationships

This Agreement does not make either party a partner, joint venturer or employee of the other party.

Explanation: _Your relationship with the developer is defined by this agreement. But to an outsider, it may appear that you have a different relationship, such as a partnership or joint venture. It's possible that an unscrupulous developer will try to capitalize on this appearance — for example, claim to be your partner to obtain a benefit from a third party._

This clause gives you a basis to pursue an unscrupulous developer who attempts to capitalize on claims of a relationship other than that defined in the agreement.

25. Invalid Provisions

If a court finds any provision of this Agreement invalid or unenforceable, the remainder of this Agreement will be interpreted so as best to carry out the parties' intent.

Explanation: _Clauses like those in sections 25 through 32 are found in many types of agreements. For more information, see_ Customizing Written Contracts _at the end of this chapter._

26. Entire Agreement

This is the entire Agreement between the parties. It replaces and supersedes any oral agreements between the parties, as well as any prior writings.

27. Modification

Any modifications to this Agreement must be in writing.

28. Waiver

The failure to exercise any right in this Agreement will not waive prior or subsequent rights.

29. Notices

All notices must be in writing. A notice may be delivered to a party at the address the party designates in writing. A notice may be delivered:

a. in person
b. by certified mail, or
c. by overnight courier.

30. Successors and Assigns

This agreement binds and benefits the heirs, successors and assigns of the parties.

31. Attorney Fees and Expenses

Explanation: *If there is litigation, the prevailing party may collect from the other party its reasonable costs and attorney fees incurred in enforcing this Agreement.*

32. Governing Law

This Agreement will be governed by and construed in accordance with the laws of the state of _____.

Explanation: *For information on signing the agreement, see Customizing Written Contracts at the end of this chapter.*

Dated: _____

CLIENT:

Name of Business: _____

A _____

By: _____

Printed Name and Title:_____

Address: _____

DEVELOPER:

Name of Business: _____

A _____

By: _____

Printed Name and Title:_____

Address: _____

Attachment 1

Development Stages and Due Dates		
Development Services will consist of four stages:		
Stage	**Services**	**Due Date**
Concept	The parties will discuss and agree upon the basic concept for the Client website and Developer will prepare a written summary of the basic elements of the website's functionality and appearance.	Within ___ days of the effective date.
Design	The parties will discuss and agree upon the design of the Client website. Developer will prepare a detailed summary of the proposed appearance, operation and functionality including a list of all necessary software and materials necessary to launch the Site.	Within ___ days of the approval of the Concept Stage.
Initial Development	Developer will prepare the following Web pages for the Site _____ _____ and demonstrate the following functionality for the Site _____.	Within ___ days of the approval of the Design Stage.
Final Development	Developer will complete all requirements for the Site and host it in a manner that Client can view it for a period of at least ___ days.	Within ___ days of the approval of the Initial Development Stage.

Development Fee

Client will pay Developer as follows:

Fee	Due Date
$_____	Within ____ days of the effective date
$_____	Upon approval of the Design Stage
$_____	Upon approval of the Initial Development Stage
$_____	Upon approval of the Final Development Stage

Dated: _____

CLIENT:

Name of Business: _____

A _____

By: _____

Printed Name and Title: _____

Address: _____

DEVELOPER:

Name of Business: _____

A _____

By: _____

Printed Name and Title: _____

Address: _____

Attachment 2

Maintenance and New Development

Following launch of the Site, Developer will provide the following services at the following rates:

Service	Rate
Technical support necessary to maintain reliable performance of the features and functionality of the Site	_____ per month
Consulting and new development services	_____ per hour

Client will pay Developer within 30 days of receiving Developer's invoice. Client grants to Developer a license to reproduce and modify the Site content to provide these services.

F. Customizing Written Contracts

Throughout this book, we offer sample contracts. To help you customize the contracts, we provide explanations and instructions where appropriate. But there are some basic concepts that apply to practically every contract. These include:

- how to name the parties at the beginning of a contract
- how to provide for resolution of disputes
- how to insert common clauses covering such things as waivers and jurisdiction, and
- how to properly sign the contract.

To avoid explaining these basic concepts over and over, we discuss them here. When similar clauses appear later in the book, we'll refer you back to these explanations.

1. Identifying the Parties to a Contract

At the beginning of a contract, you'll need to fill in the names of the individuals or businesses who are making the contract. How you identify these parties depends on the type of business entities involved. You not only need to make sure that you correctly name the business, you should also designate its legal nature —partnership or corporation, for instance.

Assume, for example, that Mary Jones, a sole proprietor, wants to create an e-commerce website. She wants to hire The Website People Inc. to develop the site for her. Website People's shareholders are Alice Appleby and Richard Reardon, who are respectively the president (Alice) and secretary-treasurer (Richard) of the corporation. How do you identify the parties at the start of the contract?

As a sole proprietor, Mary Jones can just fill in her own name. If she's using a fictitious name to operate her business—like Jones Furniture—she should add "doing business as Jones Furniture" after her name. What about the corporation? You'll need to include (1) the official corporate name, and (2) identify the state of incorporation. Thus, the correct form is "The Website People Inc., a New York Corporation."

So in our example, the first clause of the contract might read as follows:

> This Agreement is made by The Website People Inc., a New York Corporation (Developer), and Mary Jones doing business as Jones Furniture (Client).

Or, with different entities signing a similar agreement, the names would appear like this:

> This Agreement is made by Website Creation Associates, an Ohio Partnership (Developer), and ProtoBiz LLC, a Michigan Limited Liability Company (Client).

The table below gives the recommended format for the business forms you're likely to run into.

How to Identify Parties to a Contract	
Type of Entity	**Format**
Individual	John Smith
Two or More Individuals	John Smith and Mary Jones
Sole Proprietor (Either style can be used)	John Smith [or] John Smith, doing business as John's Diner
General Partnership	Smith & Jones, a Michigan Partnership
Limited Partnership	Professional Management Limited Partnership, a New York Limited Partnership
Corporation	Modern Textiles Inc., a Texas Corporation
Limited Liability Company	Games and Such LLC, a Michigan Limited Liability Company

2. Dispute Resolution Clause

It's become popular to try to solve business disputes out of court, to save time and money. However, taking a dispute out of the court system may not always be the right decision. In arbitration, for example, you'll be bound by a decision from which there is no appeal.

Our form provides a number of optional approaches to resolving disputes, should they arise.

Mediation. In mediation, a neutral facilitator (the mediator) helps the parties resolve their dispute. Both sides sit down with the mediator and tell their stories. The mediator sorts out the issues and may suggest ways to resolve the dispute. If the parties agree to a solution, they sign an enforceable settlement agreement.

Mediation is the most inexpensive and peaceable method of solving problems. You can arrive at a settlement rather than being told how to resolve the dispute by an arbitrator or judge. It's less likely to exacerbate bad feelings between the parties, as lawsuits inevitably do. Mediation, however, doesn't force parties to end the dispute. If it doesn't work, you must find some binding method of ending the battle, either arbitration or litigation.

Arbitration. Arbitration is like going to court but with less formality and expense. Instead of filing a lawsuit, the parties hire one or more arbitrators to evaluate the dispute and make a determination. The arbitration process can be relatively simple, although it usually requires some document preparation and a hearing. You don't need a lawyer to represent you, but many businesses prefer a lawyer's help in presenting the strongest legal arguments.

Occasionally, parties agree that an arbitrator's determination will be advisory, in which case either party can disregard it and file a lawsuit. Much more often, however, it's binding. It can be enforced by a court and can't be overturned unless something especially unfair happened—for example, you later learn that the arbitrator owned stock in your opponent's company.

To arbitrate a dispute, both parties must consent. Unfortunately, when you're in the midst of a dispute, it's hard to get the parties to agree to anything. So, the best method of guaranteeing arbitration is to include an arbitration provision in your contracts.

Finding a mediator or arbitrator. Many associations and companies offer mediation and arbitration services. The best-known organization is the American Arbitration Association (AAA). It has offices in every state and can provide mediators and arbitrators in most areas. To check the availability of AAA arbitrators or mediators in your area, visit http://www.adr.org.

Nolo's *How to Mediate Your Dispute: Find a Solution Quickly and Cheaply Outside the Courtroom,* by Peter Lovenheim, provides more information on mediation and arbitration.

3. Other Common Contract Clauses

Many basic clauses appear in all types of contracts. Here's what they're about.

a. Invalid Provisions

The clause that lawyers call a *severability* clause says that if you wind up in a lawsuit over the agreement and a court rules that one part of the agreement is invalid, that part can be cut out but the rest of the agreement will remain valid. If you don't include a clause like ours and some portion of your agreement is deemed invalid, then the whole agreement may be canceled.

b. Entire Agreement

In the process of negotiation and contract drafting, you and the other party may make many oral or written statements. Some of these statements make it into the final agreement. Others don't. This clause, known as an *integration clause,* verifies that the version you're signing is the final version, and that neither of you can rely on statements made in the past. *This is it!* Without an integration provision, it's possible that either party could claim rights based upon promises made before the deal was signed.

⚠️ **Watch out for "We'll fix it later" promises.** The integration clause closes the door on any oral or written promises. Don't sign an agreement if something is missing and don't accept an assurance that the other party will correct it later.

c. Modification

This clause establishes that if either party makes promises after the agreement is signed, those promises will be binding only if they're made in a signed amendment (*addendum,* in lawyer's lingo) to the agreement.

d. Waiver

This provision states that even if you don't promptly complain about a violation of the agreement, you still have the right to complain about it later. Without this kind of clause, if you know the other party has breached the agreement but you let it pass, you give up (waive) your right to sue over it. For example, imagine that the other party is supposed to use your confidential information for your site only. You're aware that the other party is violating the agreement in a minor way, but you're willing to permit it because everything else in your work with the other party is exceeding your expectations. Six months later, however, the honeymoon is over and you're no longer willing to tolerate a misuse of your confidential informa-

tion. A waiver provision allows you to sue. The other party can't defend itself by claiming it relied on your past practice of accepting its breaches. Of course, the provision swings both ways. If you breach the agreement, you can't rely on the other party's past acceptance of *your* behavior.

e.   Notices

Agreements often provide for parties to send notices to one another. There can be a question about how a notice is to be delivered if it's to be valid. Our clause suggests three ways—but if there are others that you'd like to include, such as email, just add them.

f.   Successors and Assigns

It's possible that either party will be succeeded by someone else. For example, a sole proprietor's heirs may inherit the business. In that case, you'd want to make sure that the heirs are bound by all the requirements of the agreement—such as confidentiality requirements. In other cases, a party may assign its rights to another company. For example, the other business may be sold to another company.

Our clause says that in either case, the new parties will get the benefits of the agreement—and will be bound by its requirements.

g.   Attorney Fees

What if the other party breaches the agreement and you're forced to sue? The rate for business lawyers is $200 to $400 an hour. A lawsuit can cost $5,000, $50,000 or even more, depending on the length of the suit and the subject matter. The amount you pay lawyers could quickly overshadow any amount you might win.

In the United States (unlike many other countries), the loser of a lawsuit isn't required to pay the winner's attorney fees. In other words, each party has to pay its own lawyer, regardless of how the suit turns out. There are two exceptions to this rule:

1) a court may award fees if a specific law permits it; and
2) a court must award attorney fees if a contract provides for it.

In most situations, you'll get your attorney fees paid only if you use a provision like the one in our agreement. Because lawyers are so expensive, having an attorney fee provision—that is, having each side afraid it will get stuck paying the other's attorney fees—can prove crucial to ending a dispute.

This attorney fees provision is mutual—that is, whoever wins the lawsuit is awarded attorney fees. This is fair, and encourages the quick resolution of lawsuits. One-sided provisions, no matter which side they favor, create an uneven playing field for resolving disputes. One state (California) recognizes this unfairness and automatically converts a one-way attorney fees contract provision into a mutual one.

h. Governing Law

Every state has laws regarding contract interpretation. You can choose any state's laws to govern the agreement, regardless of where you live or where the agreement is signed. Most businesses favor the state where their headquarters are located.

Does it matter which state you choose? Some states have a reputation of being favorable for certain kinds of disputes. For example, California's state and federal courts have resolved many high-tech disputes; as a body of law has developed, judges' decisions have become more predictable. Generally, however, the differences in state law are not great enough to make this a major negotiating issue.

4. Signing a Contract

For a contract to be legally binding, all parties must sign it. Signing a document seems like a simple and obvious task, but it does involve a few important legal subtleties. Let's consider what format should be used for signing the contract between Mary Jones and The Website People Inc. As sole proprietor, Mary Jones must begin with (1) the name of her business, followed by (2) the type of

business entity it is—here, a sole proprietorship—followed by (3) her signature, (4) her name printed out, (5) her title in the business—in this case, owner—and, if desired, (6) her address. Like so:

```
CLIENT

Jones Furniture
A Sole Proprietorship
By: _____
Mary Jones
Owner
1234 Lucky St.
White Plains, New York
```

The corporation includes the same information, except that someone authorized by the corporation (often, its president) must sign on behalf of the business.

```
DEVELOPER

The Creative People Inc.
A New York Corporation
By: _____
Alice Appleby
President
123 Chesterfield Boulevard
White Plains, New York
```

The table below shows you how to deal with signatures in all common business contexts.

Formats for Signatures in Legal Forms	
Type of Entity	**Signature Line**
Individual	*John Smith* John Smith
Two or More Individuals	*John Smith* John Smith *Mary Jones* Mary Jones
Sole Proprietor (Either style can be used)	*John Smith* John Smith [or] John's Diner A Sole Proprietorship By *John Smith* John Smith, Owner
General Partnership	Smith & Jones A Michigan Partnership By *Mary Jones* Mary Jones, Partner
Limited Partnership	Professional Management Limited Partnership A New York Limited Partnership By *Mary Jones* Mary Jones, General Partner
Corporation	Modern Textiles Inc. A Texas Corporation By *Mary Jones* Mary Jones, President
Limited Liability Company	Games and Such LLC A Michigan Limited Liability Company By *Mary Jones* Mary Jones, Member/Manager

Website Hosting: Putting Your Site on the Web

For visitors to reach your site, it has to be hosted on a server, a special computer that runs around the clock. A server holds many times more data than the average personal computer and has a special high-speed connection to the Internet.

Although you can buy and set up your own server, few businesses take this route because it requires considerable time, expense and maintenance. Most e-businesses prefer to pay a company that specializes in storing and maintaining websites, known as a *website host*. A website host is like a landlord who owns a building. You, along with several other companies, lease space on the host's server. The size and features of your space affect the rental price. For example, the more megabytes of storage space that you lease, or the more sophisticated the shopping cart features that you require, the more you'll pay each month for leasing space on the server.

Finding a suitable website host and transferring your site and domain name to the server requires a little technical knowledge. If you don't ask the right questions of a potential host, visitors to your site may find Web pages slow to open, or you may have difficulty later transferring the site to another host. This chapter explains how to figure out what you need from a host and how to get it for a reasonable price.

Look into website hosting early in the game. Although you don't need to sign a hosting agreement until you're ready to open your website to the general public, it makes sense to learn about hosting costs at the same time you're looking to hire a website developer. Prospective developers can help educate you about hosting and knowing all the costs upfront will let you create a realistic e-commerce budget.

A. Types of Website Hosting

In general, there are three types of website hosting: virtual, free and dedicated.

1. Virtual Hosting

For most small businesses, the most common choice for website hosting is *virtual hosting,* where you lease space on a server that's shared by several businesses. The costs range from $20 to $150 a month depending on the website-hosting plan. There are several variables in each plan, and we discuss them in Section B. A website developer—if you use one—may also be provide virtual hosting as part of its development contract. For example, for a monthly fee of $35, the developer may host and maintain your site.

2. Free Hosting

Many companies that provide access to the Web (Internet Service Providers or ISPs) offer free hosting services. Because of the limitations discussed below, free hosting—although it's fine for clubs, hobbies and friends' sites—is probably not ideal for your business.

As with most services that are "free," there's a trade-off: In order to access your site, visitors can't simply type in your domain name—for example, http://www.protobiz.com. Instead, the visitor must use a long website address supplied by the hosting service to access it—for example, http://aol.members.com/rjones/protobiz. These longer domain names are harder to remember and lack a professional ring. It is possible, however, to use your domain name by having a hosting service or domain name registration service redirect visitors who type in your domain name. This means that a Web user who types in your domain name will be transferred to your ISP-hosted site. Often, your domain name registration service will provide this re-direction service for free. Sometime there is a monthly charge of $5 or $10. In either case, the inability to directly access the site under a simple domain name may not bode well for your online image.

In addition, your free space is limited—often to two to ten megabytes. If you have only about 50 to 100 Web pages, this is fine. But if you have more—for example, if you provide large downloadable files—it may not be enough space. What's more, many features such as shopping carts, chat rooms and message boards are not available with some free sites. Finally, free hosting services usually require that you carry banner ads from their advertisers and may prohibit your use of banner ads from other advertisers.

3. Dedicated and Colocation Hosting

You can also make an arrangement with a website host to rent your own server, an arrangement known as *dedicated hosting*. In this scenario, your site is the only one on the server. You control the security and you maintain the server so you have control over its reliability. We don't recommend this route except for fairly large businesses that employ Information Technology managers—people who can manage the complicated and highly technical world of website servers.

Colocation hosting is the same as dedicated hosting except instead of renting the server from the website host, you purchase the server, maintain it and keep it with the website host's other servers.

B. Choosing a Website Host

If you conclude (as most small businesses do) that leasing space on a server makes the most sense for your website, your next task is to find the right website host. It's a good idea to ask your website developer since the choice often depends on technical matters such as the software used to create and maintain your website. Without going into the gruesome technical details, your choice may be influenced by whether or not your site:

- was written with Microsoft FrontPage
- requires an NT or UNIX servers
- requires database support
- needs a message board or other ways for visitors to converse
- will process credit card orders, and
- will contain adult content, offensive chat room activity, or send out spam email (some hosts prohibit this).

You may also get leads from friends or business associates. If you'd like to comparison shop for website hosting features, sites such as The List (http://webhosts.thelist.com) and Find Webspace (http://www.findwebspace.com) can help you identify hosts that meet your requirements.

1. Features to Look For

Chances are good you may be concerned only with a few hosting features that are included in basic and premium virtual hosting plans. These features include:

- **Disk space.** This is the amount of disk space that the host permits you to occupy on the server. As a general rule, you'll need roughly ten MB for 100 Web pages. The actual number will depend on the amount of data on each page. Graphics take more space than text does.
- **Site access.** This is the time during the day when you have access to the server to modify your site. Most plans offer around-the-clock service.
- **Email accounts.** Besides storing your site, the host will permit you to maintain email accounts for your business on the server. Basic plans usually provide five email accounts.
- **Number of visitors.** Most website hosts limit the total number of visitors to your site each month because the Web host has limited access to the Internet. Thousands of users at one time would overload the server. Usually that's not an issue for a small business starting on the Web. Most basic plans permit at least five gigabytes (GB) of data transfer. That's roughly equivalent to 60,000 page views per month which should be sufficient for your needs. (A page view refers to one visitor accessing one page—so for example, if 20,000 visitors each looked at three pages, that would be 60,000 page views.)

- **Shopping carts and credit card processing.** More extensive hosting plans offer special shopping plans—for example, manual or automatic credit card services. If you choose manual credit card services, the customer enters credit card information on your site but you'll have to individually key the information regarding each transaction and forward it to a credit card company for approval. The manual method is best if you're selling five to ten products and expect no more than about 100 transactions per month. For more on credit cards, see Chapter 10.

2. Questions to Ask the Host

In addition to querying your website host about the features discussed above, you should also get answers to the following questions. Contact other businesses that use the same host if you need to dig deeper. The website host should be able to provide you with a list.

a. Will You Get Uninterrupted Service?

Look for a website host with a reputation for providing uninterrupted service—or more precisely, service with only a few interruptions, since perfection is unheard of in this industry. A website host will have a relationship with one or more of the "backbone" carriers that provide the network that ultimately make the Internet connections. Basically, the more backbone carriers a website host is connected to, the better. Redundancy is good. If there's a service glitch on one carrier's lines, your website host can quickly shift to another carrier with which it has a working relationship. This means less downtime for your site.

The best approach would be to include, in the contract, a statement that the maximum downtime—the time when your site is not running—is 15 or 20 minutes a month. If the downtime exceeds this amount, you should get a reduction in monthly charges. Unfortunately, most website hosts have a standard contract, which contains only a vague promise to keep downtime "as low as possible," and are unwilling to commit to a specific amount.

b. Will You Get Speedy Service?

You want speedy connections—a visitor to your website won't stick around if it takes forever to connect to the site or to download pages. You need to assess the speed a website host can deliver, especially during peak times when its facilities are pushed to the max. And you need to see what kind of speed guarantees the website host's contract contains.

The standards for guaranteed speed are generally stated in technical terms. Your website developer should be able to help you understand this. Ideally, the website host should guarantee that you'll always have a stated server response time for your site.

Bandwidth is an important factor that affects speed. Think of bandwidth as the size of the electronic pipe that your site's information must pass through. If the pipe is too narrow, then information may move through it too slowly. Again, impatient users or even reasonably patient ones may abandon your site perhaps never to return again. You'd like the website host to guarantee in the contract that you have a minimum amount of bandwidth at all times.

Just as you'd like a guarantee of minimum bandwidth, the website host may want to place a cap on the upper end of how much bandwidth your monthly payment entitles you to receive. That's understandable, but if you do reach agreement on an upper limit, you'd like to know that the website host will automatically furnish additional bandwidth— which you'll pay extra for—when conditions require it. For example, if some Wednesday at 2 p.m. you get double the usual number of visitors trying to check out your site, you'd like to be sure that the website host will provide sufficient bandwidth to deal with this burst of activ-

ity so your site doesn't slow to a snail's pace.

Ideally, as with the downtime guarantees, the website host should reduce your bill if the host fails to provide the minimum bandwidth that's been promised, or doesn't come through with additional bandwidth when it's needed.

c. What Type of Support Services Will You Get?

You and your website developer should discuss the type of maintenance and support you'll need from your website host. Then, you'll want to see that the contract with the website host covers these services. For example, the host may agree to monitor your site to make sure it continues to run correctly. You'd like the host to notify you promptly if trouble arises and to put qualified technicians to work to solve the problem. (Note that this type of hosting maintenance is different than the website maintenance discussed in Chapter 3, which entails maintaining the functionality and appearance of your site.)

Also, get the name of the person you're to contact if you spot a problem with the website that the host needs to correct. It's also helpful for the contract to require the host to give you server logs monthly or weekly containing accurate information about traffic on your site, bandwidth usage and similar data.

d. How Can You End the Relationship?

You need an exit strategy, in case someday you switch to another website host. Your contract should permit you to terminate freely and without a reason. Most contracts require some notice, perhaps 30 days.

You also want an assurance in your contract that the transition will go smoothly. Ask the host to agree that if you end the hosting relationship, the host must return the website to you within a stated time period—say, 24 hours. This commitment should stay in effect even if the host believes you've breached the contract—for example, by not paying a bill on time. As we note in Section C, however, it's often difficult to get this type of promise.

One way to protect yourself is to require the website host to give you periodic backups of your site. That way, you can make a seamless shift to a new host. It's also prudent to keep a copy of everything you give the host. That way, if the relationship breaks down, you and your website developer can probably reconstruct the site at minimal expense and turn it over to a new host.

Finally, find out if the website host will provide a temporary *pointer* that directs users to your new site while you are moving from one host to another.

3. Website Host Extras

Many website hosts offer additional services you may be interested in. These often include:

- **Domain name registration.** The host will offer to register your domain name. Since it's quite simple to register your own domain name, there's no added value for this service. If the host does register your domain name, make sure that your business owns the name and you're listed as the contact person with the domain name registry. This will guarantee that you'll receive notice of when it's time to renew the name and can keep the name from lapsing.

- **Search engine submission.** For an additional fee of $20 or more, a host may offer to submit your website to search engines. Such submissions—providing domain name addresses and page titles—are intended to increase the likelihood that someone using the search engine will locate your site. There are many companies that perform similar services, sometimes for less. For more information on these services, check Search Engine Watch, at http://www.searchenginewatch.com.

- **Site modification.** Some hosts will perform developer duties such as changing pages and adding features. Whether this is an important feature for you depends on the quality and price of the maintenance.

C. The Website Hosting Contract

Once you've chosen a website host and agreed on a plan, you'll need to sign a written agreement. As mentioned earlier, most website hosts aren't willing to make significant changes to their standard contracts to accommodate the wishes of one small business.

We've pulled a typical agreement from the Web to illustrate some common contract clauses. (To see more examples, simply type "website hosting agreement" in a search engine.) Not surprisingly, these agreements lean heavily towards protecting the host, so you'll want to read and understand the conditions. And since you'll probably be stuck with the contract as-is, be sure to research the hosting company to find out about its reliability and business practices. Again, an experienced website developer can be an invaluable guide.

Website Hosting Agreement

This Agreement is between _____ (Website Host) and _____ (Client).

RECITALS:

Website Host is an information provider connected to the Internet. Website Host offers storage and transfer services over the Internet through access to its Web Server;

Client seeks to utilize Website Host's server for its own purposes;

The Internet is neither owned nor controlled by any one entity; therefore, Website Host cannot guarantee that any given reader will be able to access Website Host's server at any given time.

Website Host will make every good faith effort to ensure that its server is available as widely as possible and with as little service interruption as possible;

In consideration of the mutual promises contained herein, the parties agree as follows:

A. Financial Arrangements

1. Client agrees to a three-month contract, beginning upon Website Host's receipt of confirmation of this agreement by fax, mail or express mail. Client agrees to pay Website Host for services rendered pursuant to the payment schedule.

2. First three months payment will be due upon receipt of contract.

3. This agreement will automatically renew for successive three-month periods unless canceled in writing before the quarterly renewal date. Client will receive an invoice for charges and payment is due upon receipt.

4. Client may elect to pay annually. In that case, special discounts may apply as specified on the price sheet current at the time.

B. Taxes

Website Host will not be liable for any taxes or other fees to be paid in accordance with or related to purchases made from Client or Website Host's server. Client agrees to take full responsibility for all taxes and fees of any nature associated with such products sold.

C. Material and Products

1. Client will provide Website Host with material and data in a condition that is "server-ready," which is in a form requiring no additional manipulation on the part of Website Host. Website Host will make no effort to validate this information for content, correctness or usability.

2. Website Host will exercise no control over the content of the information passing through the network. Website Host makes no warranties or representations of any kind, whether expressed or implied for the service it is providing. Website Host also disclaims any warranty of merchantability or fitness for particular purpose and will not be responsible for any damages that may be suffered by the Client, including loss of data resulting from delays, non-deliveries or service interruptions by any cause or errors or omissions of the Client. Use of any information obtained by way of Website Host is at the Client's own risk, and Website Host specifically denies any responsibility for the accuracy or quality of information obtained through its services. Website Host does not represent guarantees of available end-to-end bandwidth. Website Host expressly limits its damages to the Client for any non-accessibility time or other down time to the prorated monthly charge during the system unavailability. Website Host specifically denies responsibility for any damages arising as a consequence of such unavailability. In the event that this material is not "Server-ready," Website Host may, at its option and at any time, reject this material, including but not limited to after it has been put on Website Host's Server. Website Host agrees to notify Client immediately of its refusal of the material and afford Client the opportunity to amend or modify the material to satisfy the needs and/or requirements of Website Host. If the Client fails to modify the material, as directed by Website Host, within a reasonable period of time, which will be determined between the parties themselves, the Agreement will be deemed to be terminated.

D. Trademarks & Copyrights

Client warrants that it has the right to use any applicable trademarks provided for its site, if any, and grants Website Host the right to use such trademarks in connection with Website Host's Server service.

E. Hardware, Equipment & Software

The customer is responsible for and must provide all telephone, computer, hardware and software equipment and services necessary to access Website Host. Website Host makes no representations, warranties or assurances that the Customer's equipment will be compatible with the Website Host service.

F. Age

The Customer certifies that he or she is at least 18 years of age.

G. Internet Etiquette

Electronic forums such as mail distribution lists and Use Net news groups all have expectations regarding subject area and appropriate etiquette for posting. Users of these forums should be considerate of the expectations and sensitivities of others on the network when posting material for electronic distribution. The network resources of Website Host may not be used to impersonate another person or misrepresent authorization to act on behalf of others or Website Host. All messages transmitted via Website Host should correctly identify the sender; users may not alter the attribution of origin in electronic mail messages or posting. Users must not attempt to undermine the security or integrity of computing systems or networks and must not attempt to gain unauthorized access.

H. Termination

Either party may terminate this Agreement, without cause, by giving the other party 30 days written notice. Notwithstanding the above, Website Host may terminate service under this Agreement at any time, with immediate effect, and without penalty, if the Client fails to comply with the terms of this Agreement. During the first 60 days the Client is entitled to a 100% money back guarantee that applies in the event the Client is dissatisfied with the service for any reason. This applies to website hosting fees, and does not apply to Web promotion, Web design, custom programming work, and set up fees other than for Website hosting, such as for shopping carts, CyberCash, Chat Rooms, Forums, etc. Nor does this apply to cancellation for reasons other than dissatisfaction with Website Host's service (e.g. Client decided to discontinue Web site for personal or business reasons).

I. Limited Liability

1. Client expressly agrees that use of Website Host's Server is at Client's sole risk. Neither Website Host, its employees, affiliates, agents, third party information providers, merchants, licensers or the like, warrant that Website Host's Server service will be uninterrupted or error free; nor do they make any warranty as to the results that may be obtained from the use of the Server service or as to the accuracy, reliability or content of any information service or merchandise contained in or provided through the Website Host Server service, unless otherwise expressly stated in this Agreement.

2. Under no circumstances, including negligence, will Website Host, its officers, agents or anyone else involved in creating, producing or distributing Website Host's Server service be liable for any direct, indirect, incidental, special or consequential damages that result from the use of or inability to use the Website Host Server service; or that results from mistakes,

omissions, interruptions, deletion of files, errors, defects, delays in operation or transmission or any failure of performance, whether or not limited to acts of God, communication failure, theft, destruction or unauthorized access to Website Host's records, programs or services. Client acknowledges that this paragraph will apply to all content on Website Host's Server service.

3. Notwithstanding the above, Client's exclusive remedies for all damages, losses and causes of actions whether in contract, tort including negligence or otherwise, will not exceed the aggregate dollar amount which Client paid during the term of this Agreement and any reasonable attorney's fee and court costs.

J. Lawful Purpose

Client may only use Website Host's Server for lawful purpose. Transmission of any material in violation of any Federal, State or Local regulation is prohibited. This includes, but is not limited to material that infringes copyrights or is material legally judged to be threatening or obscene. Use of Website Host's facilities for bulk email of any kind (spam or UCE) is expressly prohibited.

K. Indemnification

Client agrees that it will defend, indemnify, save and hold Website Host harmless from any and all demands, liabilities, losses, costs and claims, including reasonable attorneys' fees ("Liabilities") asserted against Website Host, its agents, its customers, servants officers and employees, that may arise or result from any service provided or performed or agreed to be performed or any product sold by Client, its agents, employees or assigns. Client agrees to defend, indemnify and hold harmless Website Host against Liabilities arising out of (i) any injury to person or property caused by any products sold or otherwise distributed in connection with Website Host's Server; (ii) any material supplied by Client infringing or allegedly infringing on the proprietary rights of a third party; (iii) copyright infringement; and (iv) any defective product which Client sold on Website Host Server.

L. Bandwidth Limitations

Website Host does not enforce any quota limits on bandwidth per client. However, Website Host reserves the right to revise this policy on a commercial basis. In the event the policy is revised, client will have at least 30 days advance notice of such changes in Website Host's policy.

This Agreement constitutes the entire understanding of the parties. Any changes or modifications thereto must be in writing and signed by both parties.

This Agreement shall be governed and construed in accordance with the laws of the State of California.

IN WITNESS WHEREOF, the parties hereto have executed this agreement as of the date indicated below.

_____

Client—Sign, Print Name & Date

_____

Website Host

Avoiding Problems With Content on Your Site

E-commerce sites use text, photos and graphics, even audio and video, to attract and maintain customers. Because it's so easy to cut and paste text or images from someone else's website, you may be tempted to build your site that way. As you'll see in this chapter, you need to fight the temptation.

Using OPM—Other People's Material—can lead to serious legal problems. This content may be protected under copyright or trademark law. If you don't have the right to use it, you could get sued, and have to remove the content from your site and pay damages for your wrongful use. The easiest way to avoid problems is to get permission from the owner to use the work, as explained in this chapter. We also explain privacy and defamation principles so that you can avoid pitfalls when using a person's name or image.

A. Copyright Basics

Most of the problems discussed in this chapter arise when someone violates copyright law, so let's start with a quick overview. Copyright law protects music, architecture, writing, computer programs, plays, movies, dance or visual arts such as graphic arts, sculptures, photographs or paintings. The person (or business) that creates a copyrightable work is known as an author, and is the only one

who has the right to publish the material. An author can register a copyright with the federal Copyright Office, but copyright law protects authors even without registration. Registration is a good idea, though, because it enhances the value of a copyright and provides benefits if there's a lawsuit.

Copyright protection begins once a work is created and generally lasts for the life of the author plus 70 years for works created by a single author. Other works are protected for 120 years from date of creation or 95 years from first publication, whichever is longer.

Other people probably own the copyright on most items you'd consider using on your website, such as newspaper or magazine articles, product descriptions from an advertising brochure, long passages from a book, music, photographs, paintings or drawings. But there are limitations on copyright—for example, it does not protect facts and ideas, only how facts and ideas are expressed. So you're free to adapt facts and ideas from another source, as long as you put them in your own words.

> **EXAMPLE:** Roberta sells garden supplies online. To keep customers coming back to her website, she offers useful gardening advice. Roberta learns—from a copyrighted book— that a certain type of plant grows best in direct sunlight and requires a lot of

water. She's free to state those facts in her own words, without fear of infringing on the copyright of the book's author or publisher.

Copyright also does not protect short phrases such as "Show me the money!" or "Beam me up." These short phrases, names, titles or groups of words are considered common idioms of the English language and are free to all. However, these short phrases may be protected under trademark law. (See Section E.)

B. Determining Whether or Not You Need Permission

You can own or acquire ownership of copyrighted material in three ways:

- You create it
- You have it created as a work made for hire, or
- You buy the copyright from its owner.

Generally, if you haven't acquired copyright in one of these ways, you'll need permission to use someone else's creative material on your website. There are, however, a few exceptions. Sometimes you can reproduce a photograph, a song or text without authorization—for example, if the work has fallen into the "public domain"—that is, it's no longer protected by copyright. (See Section B3.) You may also borrow material under the "fair use" doctrine. (See Section B4.)

It's always safest, though, to assume you need permission and to ask for it. Getting permission usually isn't difficult or expensive; the fee for common text, photo or artwork uses is commonly under $150 per use, and in some cases, it's free.

If you use other people's work without consent, the more successful your site becomes, the more likely that the copyright owner will learn of your unauthorized use. And the legal fees you'll pay to defend yourself against a charge of unauthorized use will be ten to 50 times the average permission expense—or more.

In general, the permissions process involves five simple steps:

1. Determine if permission is needed.
2. Determine the rights you need.
3. Identify the owner.
4. Contact the owner and negotiate payment (if any).
5. Get your permission agreement in writing.

The rest of this section explains how to determine if permission is needed to use content. Section C covers how to get permission.

1. Material You Created

If you're the creator of an original work—whether it's text, an image, music, animation or any of the common elements of a website—you're the copyright owner and have the exclusive right to reproduce, distribute or adapt it or, in the case of a play, movie or musical composition, to publicly perform it. The copyright lasts for your life plus 70 years. You can assign these rights or license some or all of them to someone else.

Copyright law protects a work from the moment it's created. You don't have to register the work or use a copyright notice to obtain copyright protection although, as explained in Section A, it's sometimes beneficial to do so.

2. Material You Paid Someone to Create

If you pay someone to create a work for you, the resulting work may qualify as a *work made for hire*. In that case, you— the hiring party—are considered the author, and you own the copyright. If it's not a work made for hire, the creator of the work—the person you paid—is the copyright owner. In that case, you can acquire ownership through an assignment.

The rules operate differently depending on whether the creator is an employee or an independent contractor.

a. Content Created by Employees

An employer *always* owns copyrightable works—for example, software programs, articles, photos, artwork and music—that are created by an employee within the scope of the employment. The employer is considered the author of the work. The copyright lasts for 95 years from publication or 120 years from creation, whichever is shorter.

EXAMPLE: Jim is an employee of ProtoBiz. The company asks him to write several consumer information pages for its website. As Jim's employer, ProtoBiz owns the copyright in the material Jim writes. It can prevent Jim from using the material himself or selling it to someone else.

If a copyrightable work isn't within the scope of employment, the employee owns it.

EXAMPLE: Jim writes a novel while on vacation. Jim owns the copyright in the novel. If ProtoBiz wants to use excerpts of the novel at its website, the company will need permission from Jim.

b. Content Created by Contractors

The copyright rules for independent contractors are different from those that apply to employees. A project created for you by an independent contractor is often called a *commissioned work*. You can only claim a commissioned work as being made-for-hire (which makes you the copyright owner) if you have a work-made-for-hire agreement in writing and it's for one of the following purposes:

- a contribution to a collective work such as a website, periodical, anthology or encyclopedia in which a number of separate contributions are assembled;
- a part of a motion picture, animation or other audiovisual work;
- a translation;
- a supplementary work such as an introduction or commentary to a work;
- a compilation;
- an instructional text that's used in day-to-day teaching activities;
- a test or answer material for a test; or
- an atlas.

Since it's not always clear whether a work fits in one of these categories, you should still protect yourself with a written agreement. In your contract with the person you commission to create the work, include a provision such as the one below. It states that if the work doesn't fall in one of the categories, the contractor assigns (transfers) ownership to you.

Sample Language for Work-for-Hire Agreement

Contractor acknowledges that the work commissioned by ProtoBiz under this contract will be deemed "work made for hire" and the property of ProtoBiz. To the extent the work commissioned does not qualify as a work made for hire, Contractor assigns to ProtoBiz all right, title and interest in the copyright to the work and all renewals and extensions of the copyright that may be secured under the laws of the United States of America and any other countries. Contractor agrees to cooperate with ProtoBiz and to sign and deliver all papers necessary to vest in ProtoBiz all rights to the work.

Hiring Independent Contractors: The Employer's Legal Guide, by Stephen Fishman (Nolo), explains whether a worker is an employee or independent contractor and includes independent contractor agreements that deal with additional issues.

3. Material That's Not Protected by Copyright

Although you should generally assume that you need permission to use existing material, there are a few limited exceptions.

Some works—such as works published in the U.S. before 1923—are not protected by copyright. They are in the "public domain," which means they're free for all to use without permission.

> **EXAMPLE:** Bill wants to include his recording of the song "Give My Regards to Broadway" on his website. Because the song was first published in 1904, it's in the public domain, and Bill can use it without seeking permission.

Trying to sort out what's in the public domain and what isn't can get very tricky and, frankly, it's often not worth the effort. Start with the presumption that, if the creative work you want to use was first published after 1922, copyright law protects it. A work published after 1922 is in the public domain only if:

- the owner of a work made a mistake (such as failing to renew the copyright);
- the work doesn't meet the minimum standards for copyright protection (such as facts, unfixed works or short phrases); or

- A U.S. government employee or officer created the work.

> **EXAMPLE:** Roberta discovers an excellent booklet from the U.S. Environmental Protection Agency that describes the safe use of pesticides. She can post the entire booklet on her garden supply website without any copyright problem.

Publications of state and local governments may or may not be protected by copyright. Check before borrowing those materials for your website.

The Public Domain: How to Find & Use Copyright-Free Writings, Music, Art & More, by Stephen Fishman (Nolo), explains how to identify public domain material.

4. Material You Make "Fair Use" Of

A copyright law principle known as *fair use* permits you to copy small portions of a work for certain purposes such as scholarship or commentary. For example, under the fair use doctrine, you could reproduce a few lines of a song in a music review without getting permission from whoever owns the copyright in the song.

Millions of dollars in legal fees have been spent attempting to define what qualifies as a fair use. There are no definites, only general rules and varying court decisions. That's because the judges and lawmakers who created the fair use exception didn't want to limit the definition of fair use. They wanted it—like free speech—to have an expansive meaning that could be open to interpretation.

Some examples of fair use are:

- quotation of excerpts in a review or criticism for purposes of illustration or comment;
- use in a parody of some of the content of the work parodied;
- summary of an address or article, with brief quotations, in a news report;
- reproduction by a teacher or student of a small part of a work to illustrate a lesson; or
- reproduction of a work in legislative or judicial proceedings or reports.

If you decide to use existing material on your site and hope to be protected by the fair use doctrine, your best bet is to keep it short. Make it clear that you're quoting and be sure to acknowledge the source. And don't sell the fair use material to anyone.

For more information on copyright law, see *The Copyright Handbook: How to Protect & Use Written Works,* by Stephen Fishman (Nolo).

C. How to Get Permission to Use Content

Once you've determined that you need permission to include something on your website, your next steps are clear.

1. Determine the Rights You Need

Begin by identifying the rights you need. Each copyright owner controls a bundle of rights related to the work, including the right to reproduce, distribute and modify the work. Because so many rights are associated with copyrighted works, you must specify the ones you need. This can be as simple as stating your intended use—for example, to reproduce a photograph in your magazine.

Asking for the proper rights can be a balancing act. You don't want to pay for more than you need, but you don't want to have to return for a second round of permissions. Sometimes this requires negotiating with the rights owner to find a middle ground for fees.

Your permission agreement will also need to deal with two other variables: exclusivity and term.

a. Exclusive or Nonexclusive

Permission is either exclusive or nonexclusive. It's exclusive if you're the only person who has the right to use the work as described in your permission agreement. Most permission requests are non-exclusive, which means that others can use the material in the same way as you can. For example, if you have a nonexclusive agreement to use a photo on your website, the same photo could be used with permission at someone else's website.

b. Term of Use

The length of time that the use is allowed is called the *term*. Your rights under a permission agreement will often be limited in duration. For example, the permission agreement in Section C4, below, is for the right to display a photograph on a website for two years. If there's no express limitation on the use, you can use the material for as long as you want or until the copyright owner revokes the permission.

2. Identify the Owner

Before you can ask for permission, you've got to find out who owns the material you want to use. Sometimes, this task is simple. Often, you may be able to locate the owner just by looking at the copyright notice on the work. For example, if the notice reads "Copyright 1998 Jones Publishing," you'd start by locating Jones Publishing. Sometimes, more research is required. Copyright ownership may have passed through several hands since your copy of the work was published. You may need to research the records at the Copyright Office website (http://www.loc.gov/copyright/search).

In addition, some kinds of art, such as film and recorded music, can involve multiple owners—each with a separate right to different underlying works. For example, to use a Johnny Cash recording, you'd have to obtain permission from the record company, the music publisher (the owner of the song) and in some cases from Mr. Cash himself.

The method of identifying owners differs from industry to industry. For example, photographic reproduction rights are often owned by stock photo organizations—for example, see The Picture Collection (http://www.thepicturecollection.com) or Corbis (http://www.corbis.com); collectives known as performing rights societies own music performance rights—for example, see BMI's site (http://www.bmi.com) or ASCAP (http://www.ascap.com). If you'd like permission to use some great cartoons on your site, check out *The New Yorker's* Cartoon Bank (http://cartoonbank.com).

Getting Permission: How to License & Clear Copyrighted Materials Online & Off, by Richard Stim (Nolo), explains more about locating copyright owners and acquiring permission.

3. Contact the Owner

Sometimes, the owner of the copyrighted material won't require payment if the portion you want to use is quite small or the owner wishes to contribute to an educational or nonprofit effort. In some cases, an artist or musician eager for exposure may agree to give you permission for free unless the work becomes profitable, or may condition payment on other factors.

> **EXAMPLE:** Sam's online business sells vintage keyboard instruments, and he wants to include some photographs of old accordions he found in a book. He contacts the copyright owner of the photographs (in this case, the photographer), who grants permission to use the photos in return for a credit at the website and a link to the photographer's website. However, the agreement also provides that if the photographs are used in a documentary film that Sam is planning, an additional one-time payment of $1,500 must be made.

Some types of permission almost always require payment. For example, using a photo owned by a stock photo agency usually costs $100 or more. But the price depends on the use you're going to make of the material. Commercial uses, such as advertisements, cost more than nonprofit or educational uses. The fees for website uses generally depend upon on the number of visitors to the site, but you should expect to pay a minimum of $50 or more for each copyright permission—for example, for the use of an article from a magazine or newspaper.

Here is an example of a basic permission request letter. The actual permission agreement would be negotiated and signed later.

Letter Requesting Permission

Dear Ms. Hitchcock:

I am writing to you about your article, "Why I Hate Surround Sound." *New Audio* Magazine informed me that you are the owner of rights in the article. I operate a website that sells audio equipment (http://www.HearRight.com) and I'd like to use an abridged version of the article at the site. The details are as follows:

Title of Your Article (the "Selection"): "Why I Hate Surround Sound"

Author: Michelle Hitchcock

Source of Article: *New Audio* Magazine

Volume, Issue, *ISSN:* Vol 23, No. 6, ISSN 1099-8722

Number of Pages: 4

My intended use of the Selection is as follows:

Rights Needed: 1) the right to shorten or modify the Selection (I'll send you a copy of the abridged version for your approval); and 2) the nonexclusive right to reproduce the Selection at the Hear Right website.

Projected Loading Date: September, 2002

I'm seeking these rights for my company, Hear Right, and for any company that might later acquire ownership of my company. Please review this request and let me know the terms for licensing rights as well as the required credit. Once you let me know, I can prepare a permission agreement.

Sincerely,

Roberta Weston

---

4. Get Your Permission Agreement in Writing

In a permission agreement (also called a license), the owner of a copyrighted work—a photo, text or music, for example—authorizes you to use it on your website. Without such permission, the copyright owner can sue for the unauthorized use of the work, referred to as infringement.

A permission agreement doesn't have to be long or complicated. Here's a sample form that might work for you if a photographer is granting you the right to use a set of photos on your website.

Permission Agreement

ProtoBiz, a Massachusetts Limited Liability Company (Protobiz) and Gregory Wolf (Photographer) agree as follows:

Photographer grants to ProtoBiz a nonexclusive license to display on its protobiz.com website the ten photographs attached to this agreement.

Within 30 days after both parties have signed this agreement, ProtoBiz will pay Photographer a fee of $500.

ProtoBiz will acknowledge Photographer as the creator of the photographs by including the following credit on the website adjacent to each photograph: Photo by Gregory Wolf (Copyright 20XX by Gregory Wolf).

This license will expire on December 31, 20XX.

Photographer warrants that he alone created the photographs and that he owns all copyright and other intellectual property rights in the photographs.

Photographer warrants that the photographs and their use on the ProtoBiz website will not violate the rights of any third parties including, but not limited to, any claims of copyright infringement, defamation or invasion of privacy.

ProtoBiz LLC

By: _____, Manager

Date: _____

_____

Gregory Wolf

Photographer

Date: _____

The warranty statements in the agreement provide an assurance that the person granting permission owns the rights being granted. The photographer guarantees that the work isn't taken from another source. If the photographer is incorrect and someone else, claiming to own the copyright, sues you for infringement and wins, the photographer will be responsible for any losses you suffer.

D. How to Buy the Rights to Copyrighted Material

An assignment is a transfer of all rights in a copyrighted work. Consider it as an alternative to getting permission. You should seek an assignment if you want to control all uses of the material. For example, you should get an assignment if an advertising agency creates a banner advertisement for your website or if a photographer shoots a series of images to use on your site. In general, we recommend getting an assignment whenever you commission someone to create art, text, music or photos for your business's use or whenever you cannot acquire rights under a work made for hire arrangement (see Section B2).

Although an assignment is a transfer of ownership, it may not last for the full term of copyright protection. The creator or the heirs of a creator of a work can recapture the copyright 35 years from the date of the assignment. For example, an independent contractor who assigned rights to a photo in 2000 can reclaim the rights in 2035. This recapture right is usually not important because few works will have a useful economic life on the Internet for more than 35 years.

You can make an assignment a matter of public record by filing it with the U.S. Copyright Office. There is no legal requirement that an assignment be recorded. The basic recording fee for a document covering no more than one title is $50. For information about recording assignments, check the Copyright Office website http://www.loc.gov/copyright or call the Copyright Office's Public

Information Office at 202-679-0700, or the Certification and Documents office at 202-707-6850. The assignment and fee should be mailed to Documents Unit LM-462, Cataloging Office, Library of Congress, Washington, DC 20559.

The basic copyright assignment that follows can be used for any type of work. More specific assignments for musicians and artists are included in *Getting Permission,* by Richard Stim (Nolo).

The Basic Copyright Assignment is on the Forms CD under the file name Assignment.RTF.

Assignment

I, _____ ("Assignor"), am the owner of the work entitled

_____ (the "Work") and described as follows:

_____ .

In consideration of $ _____ and other valuable consideration, paid by

_____ ("Assignee"), I assign to Assignee and Assignee's heirs and assigns, all

my right, title and interest in the copyright to the Work and all renewals and extensions of

the copyright that may be secured under the laws of the United States of America and any

other countries. I agree to cooperate with Assignee and to execute and deliver all papers

necessary to vest all rights to the Work.

Date: _____

[Signature of assignor(s)]

_____

Explanation: In the first paragraph, insert the assignor's name (usually the creator) and the title of the work. In the next blank space, either describe the work or enter "See attached Exhibit A" and attach a copy of the work to the assignment. In the next paragraph, insert the amount of the payment and the name of the assignee. The assignor must sign the agreement. If the agreement will be notarized, the assignor should wait to sign the agreement until there's a notary present to fill out the rest of the notary section. We recommend notarization; it provides verification of the signature and identity of the person signing the agreement.

The Facts on Clip Art

Pre-packaged clip art can be a real money-saver since, once you buy the package, you usually don't have to pay royalties—continuing payments based upon the number of reproductions— each time you to use the art. But some clip art distributors place limitations on commercial reproduction, so read the rules in the shrink-wrap agreement (the terms stuffed into the packaging) or click-wrap agreement (the terms you click to accept when you download a product or start to use it). If you have doubts, contact the copyright owner for written clarification and permission, if required.

E. Avoiding Problems When You Use Other Companies' Trademarks

A trademark is a word, phrase, symbol or design that identifies a product or service. The owner of a trademark can prevent other businesses from using that mark (or a similar one) in a way that's likely to confuse consumers about the source of a product or service. The owner also can prevent others from tarnishing the trademark and diluting its value. (If your domain name is too similar to another company's trademark, that can cause problems, too; see Chapter 2.)

1. When It's OK to Use Another's Trademark

In general, it's safe to use another company's trademark in your website in these ways:

- **Naming a trademarked product or service that you're selling.** If you're selling IBM computers or Sony TV sets, you're free to specify the brand name on your website—as long as you don't create the misleading impression that your site is run or endorsed by IBM or Sony.

- **Comparing products or services.** If you make wood patio furniture, you can compare it to a trademarked brand of outdoor furniture made by another company. Or if you administer employee tax and benefit programs, you can compare your services to those offered by a competitor, including a mention of the competitor's service mark. But of course, anytime you make comparisons, make sure they're accurate.

- **Using trademarks to provide information.** Uses that inform, educate or express opinions are protected under the First Amendment of the United States Constitution and don't require permission. For example, you don't need permission to use the Chevrolet logo in an article on a website describing Chevrolet trucks, even if the article is critical of the company. Similarly, if your site documents the history of American trucks, you won't need permission to include the Chevrolet logo. However, the use of the logo must have some relevance to the work. For example, it wouldn't be wise to publish an article critical of overseas auto manufacturing practices and include the Chevrolet logo unless Chevrolet were mentioned in the article.

Keep in mind, however, that even if you're legally entitled to use a trademark, that doesn't mean that the trademark owner will always be agreeable. If you're forced into court to prove that your use is allowed by law, in a sense you've already lost the battle. So take care to make sure your use is clearly within the bounds of the law, and carefully weigh the benefits of using the trademark if you suspect the owner will fight you with legal action.

Remember also, that what might be permitted under trademark law might not be permitted under copyright law. So if the trademark contains some copyrightable elements, analyze your use under both trademark and copyright rules.

EXAMPLE: The Sweet Sam Doll Company uses a copyrighted image of its best-selling Sweet Sam doll in its company trademark. Although under trademark law, ProtoBiz has the right to reproduce the trademark in an informational article about the doll industry, ProtoBiz may not have the right under copyright laws to reproduce the image of the doll incorporated within the trademark.

2. Don't Create Confusion Among Customers

The key rule for avoiding trademark infringement problems is: Don't make it likely that customers will be confused about the source of the goods, services or information you're promoting. If you ignore that rule, the trademark owner may take legal action to shut you down and collect damages.

EXAMPLE: Andy starts a business to repair Dell computers and sets up a website to reach customers. He names his site http:// www.dellrepairservice.com. Andy displays the Dell logo prominently on every page and includes pictures of Dell computers. He offers to send visitors an email newsletter called *Dell Details*, and he provides a link to the Dell Computer Corporation site. Because it's likely that many customers will be confused and a significant number will conclude that they're dealing with a Dell-sponsored company, Andy can expect to receive a cease-and-desist letter from Dell Computer Corporation—and, if he doesn't change his website pronto, probably a lawsuit as well.

Check your website content carefully to make sure that visitors won't be confused about who maintains the site and where the goods and services you're offering originated. If there's any room at all for customer confusion, post a prominent disclaimer making it clear that you're not affiliated with or endorsed by the business that owns the trademark or service mark in question. A disclaimer is not a cure-all, but it may help if you're later dragged into a dispute. It's also a good idea to specifically state who does own the trademarks mentioned in your site. For example, you might post a statement that "IBM is a registered trademark of the IBM Corporation."

F. Avoiding Other Content Problems

In addition to copyright and trademark concerns, you need to be aware of other possible legal surprises. If you step over the legal line in any of the following areas, the consequences can be costly.

1. Using Individuals' Names or Images to Sell Something

The First Amendment allows you to use a person's name or picture in a news story without getting permission. But that doesn't mean you can use a name or picture to promote the sale of goods or services. Basically, if you try to profit from the commercial value of someone else's identity, the person may object. The protection is broad. It applies to a person's name, nickname, image, voice and even his or her persona—intangible but recognizable characteristics associated with the person. And in most states, these rights continue even after the person has died.

> **EXAMPLE:** To promote a new line of stylish men's hats, savoirfaireclothes.com features a picture of the late Frank Sinatra on its home page. Savoirfaire doesn't have permission to post the picture. The singer's estate sends the website owner a strongly worded letter demanding that the picture be removed.

Usually, only famous people—or their heirs—complain about the commercial use of a name or image, but the legal principle applies to everyone. So if you're going to put people's names or pictures on your e-commerce website, get written permission first. Similarly, if you're licensing photos from a photographer who owns the copyright to the pictures, make sure the photographer got a release from the people in the pictures.

2. Invading Someone's Privacy

In creating your website content, you must be careful not to invade anyone's right to privacy. The law recognizes several ways that you can invade a person's right to be left alone, including:

- **False light.** This type of invasion of privacy occurs when an individual is falsely portrayed in a highly offensive manner—for example, if a website posts a composite photo that combines a woman's face with someone else's naked body.
- **Disclosure of private facts.** This invasion of privacy occurs when private or embarrassing facts are disclosed about an individual without relation to a legitimate public concern. For

example, a website publishes the fact that Don served time for a robbery 20 years earlier—even though Don has rehabilitated himself and is now a pastor. Publication of the stale information is an invasion of privacy unless there's a related public interest—for example, the pastor has again been arrested for a crime. However, with public figures such as politicians and media stars, almost everything about them can be safely disclosed.

- **Intrusion.** This means intruding upon a person in a situation in which that person has a reasonable expectation of privacy—for example, secretly setting up a webcam at someone's home.

However, it's not an invasion of privacy to photograph someone in a public place or at any event where the public is invited. Such photos can be used freely for informational purposes, if the use doesn't portray the person in a false light.

3. Damaging Someone's Reputation

Your website content can get you into legal trouble if it contains false statements that injure someone's reputation—statements that reduce people's respect for or confidence in that person. For example, a statement on your site that the owner of a competing business had been convicted of fraud would be defamatory if it weren't true. If your site does contain such statements, the injured person may sue you for defamation.

Of course, it's highly unlikely that your e-commerce site would resort to personal attacks to promote your goods or services. But if your site is engaged primarily in supplying information rather than marketing goods or services, you need to carefully screen the information you post to make sure it doesn't contain anything defamatory. When you get information from outside sources, read it carefully for defamatory content before you post it. The fact that someone else wrote the material won't generally protect you from legal liability if you publish it on your site.

Federal law does provide some protection from defamation lawsuits to Internet Service Providers (ISPs) that serve mainly as carriers of information. The theory is that these providers are similar to the Post Office; they just carry other people's messages. But that protection isn't broad enough to cover the typical business website. If you post content from outside sources—and especially if you have a bulletin board or chat room feature on your site—assume you'll be fully liable for any defamatory content.

You may need a lawyer to decide if a statement is defamatory. The tests for what's defamatory and what isn't are often difficult to apply. If you're uneasy, run the questionable content by a lawyer experienced in defamation law. Or simply err on the side of caution and don't post it.

The term defamation usually applies to statements about a person, not a business. But that doesn't mean you can safely badmouth a business. If your website says negative things about a business or its products or services, you may get sued for "disparagement."

EXAMPLE: Bill has a website for his landscape business called forevergreen.com. He posts two photos on his site. One shows a lush green lawn installed by his company. The other shows a scraggly, brownish lawn that, the site says, was planted by Bill's competitor, Stan. In fact, the second photo shows a lawn in a different city planted by an unknown landscaper. Stan sues Bill for business disparagement. ■

Posting Your Business Policies

Every business has rules for its customers. In the brick-and-mortar world, these terms and conditions can be found in a "Sorry, No Refunds" sign behind a cash register or in the legal jargon on the back of an order form. In the e-commerce world, posting terms and conditions on your website is the simple and practical equivalent. You may call them *Terms and Conditions, User Agreement, Customer Information* or *Terms of Service*. Whatever label you choose, you're largely free to craft terms and conditions to fit your specific needs.

Your terms and conditions may include three forms of legal information: transaction conditions, disclaimers and proprietary notices.

- **Transaction conditions** are the terms for doing business with you. For example, you might want to announce that your business won't accept returns more than 30 days after purchase. Your privacy policy may also be of great interest to customers.
- **Disclaimers** are statements in which you tell customers that you won't be liable for certain kinds of losses they might incur. For example, a photo developing website may disclaim responsibility for losses that result if a customer's film is lost in the mail.
- **Proprietary notices** are statements that proclaim the legal status of your intangible business assets. For example, a trademark notice lets users

know that you're claiming trademark rights in your name or logo.

Even though the customer doesn't sign on the dotted line, the posted provisions are usually legally enforceable by the business or its customers. If you want to highlight terms that are especially important, and be surer that courts will honor your fine print, you can require visitors or customers to click an "I Accept" or "I Agree" button.

Have a lawyer review or help you draft your postings. Every online business is different. An experienced business lawyer who's worked with other online companies should be able to shape the language to help it withstand a legal challenge. The most cost-effective way to get the job done is to create your own version of what you'd like to post, and then seek a lawyer's help in developing the final version.

A. Why Bother to Post Policies?

With just one major exception, there's no law requiring a website to post a set of terms and conditions or, if you do post them, how and where they should appear. The exception: the Children's Online Privacy Protection Act (COPPA) which requires you to post a privacy policy if your website is directed to children (see Chapter 12).

If you surf the Web frequently, you're probably aware that many businesses don't post their terms and conditions at all, or put them in impenetrable verbiage in an obscure location on the site. But many consumer-respected sites do display clear, fair policies. That's the direction we recommend.

Posting notices conspicuously offers both business and legal benefits. On the business side, being straight with visitors and customers builds trust, credibility and loyalty—all of which can help your online business grow.

On the legal side, a well-thought-out set of terms and conditions can help you:

- Protect your trademarks and your copyrighted content
- Limit your legal liability to customers and others, and
- Avoid disputes over the details of transactions with customers.

It's true that if a customer sues you, your terms and conditions may not give you 100% protection, but at least you and your lawyer will have some solid arguing points to present to the court.

B. What Policies to Include

Some e-commerce websites use a lengthy statement of terms and conditions; other sites have short warnings or notices linked to their home page. The amount of fine print you should have depends on your site. As a general rule, you should always include a copyright and trademark notice (see Section C). You may also want to include some of the other terms and conditions in Sections D, E and F. Here are some suggestions for the common types of e-commerce sites.

- **Business promotion.** If your site is primarily an advertisement for a brick-and-mortar business—for example, a local florist's website that provides directions to its store—you'll only need to post copyright and trademark notices.
- **Chats and posts.** If your site includes chats or postings—for example, an online tutoring website that posts student comments—you'll want to minimize your liability from illegal postings or offensive chat room comments. See Section D.
- **Information.** If your site provides consumer information—for example a local nursery's website that displays an encyclopedia of gardening—you'll want to disclaim liability for the use of the information ("We cannot guarantee our gardening advice ..."). You'll also want to disclaim liability resulting from any links you provide. See Section F6.
- **Selling.** If your site sells things, your terms and conditions become more complex. You may need notices re-

garding credit card use, warranties, refunds and returns (see Section E3), and jurisdiction and disputes (see Section F).

In addition to the terms, conditions and other notices described in this chapter, you should post a policy detailing what you do with any private information you gather when a customer visits your site or completes a transaction. See Chapter 12 for details.

Looking for examples? If you'd like to look at some sites that use terms and conditions well, consider the following: For chat room guidelines see Yahoo!Chat (http://chat.yahoo.com). For information sites, see WebMD (http://www.webmd.com) and MSNBC (http://www.msnbc.com). A good example of terms and conditions for a sales site can be found at Amazon.com (http://www.amazon.com).

Writing the Fine Print for Fine Art

When Peter Scheer and Thomas Reynolds sat down to create the terms and conditions for their fine-art site—http://www.yourwall.com—they had two lawyers at the table: themselves. Being lawyers by training, they figured they could write the necessary legal provisions to stay out of hot water. A key goal was to be clear and concise.

"We tried for a minimum of legalese," says Scheer, who manages the business. "Even so, we thought we were being too lawyerly, so we labeled that page, *Our Lawyers Made Us Do It.*

About the only thing that Scheer and Reynolds thought was important was to protect the copyrights of the pictures on the website. "Anything more was just silly because we knew that anybody who actually bought something from us

would be entering into a contract at that time, and so there'd be an opportunity then to cover any issues or liabilities that weren't addressed in our online terms and conditions."

Other issues that yourwall.com needed to make clear to its particular clientele were that:

- It would take time to get a print, because each one was made as a special order.
- The customer could reject the print for any reason for a period of time.

Beyond that, the partners decided not to worry too much.

Scheer and Reynolds also saved on lawyer fees by checking out what the competition had done. "We had the benefit of them spending money on their lawyers," Scheer says.

C. Copyright, Trademark and Patent Notices

While the Web makes it possible for you to reach millions of potential customers, it also creates the possibility that one of those visitors will make off with some of your intellectual property. A good copyright and trademark notice may help you prevent that. So can a patent notice.

1. Copyrights and Trademarks

Whether your site is a simple one-page advertisement for your local shop or a complex maze of pages selling dozens of products, you want to minimize the chances of anyone stealing any of your copyrighted content or infringing your trademarks. You own the copyright to any material you created for your site, and in many cases, you own the copyright for material that was created for you, including words, pictures, sounds or any combination of them. (For more on copyrights and website content, see Chapter 5.)

You own the copyright even if you don't put a copyright notice ("Copyright © 2002 by ProtoBiz.com LLC") on the material or don't register your copyright with the U.S. Copyright Office. Still, there are two excellent reasons to include a copyright notice on your copyrightable works.

One reason is that if someone uses copyrighted material without permission, and you sue over it, the person may claim that because there was no copyright notice, he or she didn't know the work was protected by copyright. If the judge or jury believes this, the infringer may still be liable to you, but the damages (monetary compensation) the infringer is required to pay may be drastically reduced from what they otherwise would have been. On the other hand, if there is a valid copyright notice on the work, the infringer cannot claim innocence, and you'll probably collect more damages.

The second reason for including a notice is simple: deterrence. A potential infringer may be less likely to copy if a copyright notice is posted prominently.

For similar reasons, properly written terms and conditions can also protect your trademark or service mark rights. A trademark is any word, phrase, symbol or design that identifies a product brand. A service mark identifies the provider of a service. (For more on trademarks, see Chapter 5.)

Consider covering copyrights and trademarks with something like the following:

In addition to including copyright and trademark information in your terms and conditions, it's also a good idea to put a notice on the bottom of each page of your website, similar to this one:

© 2002 by ProtoBiz.com LLC. ProtoBiz, ProtoBiz.com and ProtoBuzz are registered trademarks of ProtoBiz.com LLC.

The policies provided in this chapter are on the Forms CD under the file name Policies.RTF.

2. Patents

If your website includes a method or process that has received a patent or is the subject of a pending patent application, you should include a proprietary notice similar to this one:

The following United States patents apply to this site: [Patent Numbers]

or

The following patents are pending for this site: [Application Serial Numbers]

D. Policies for Chat Rooms and Postings

Here are terms and conditions you can use if your website lets users post information or chat.

1. Information Posted by Others

Does your website post information that's supplied by users? If so, you may want to disclaim your liability to a visitor who relies on that information. A disclaimer can help to protect you from liability to someone who relies on bad information or advice that's posted on your site.

Here's what a disclaimer might look like:

DISCLAIMER: Information Posted by Others

People other than ProtoBiz employees supply some of the content on this site. ProtoBiz has no more editorial control over such content than does a public library, bookstore or newsstand. Any opinions, advice or statements expressed by other parties are those of the others and not of ProtoBiz. ProtoBiz doesn't endorse and isn't responsible for the accuracy or reliability of any opinion, advice or statement made on the site by anyone other than authorized ProtoBiz employees while acting in their official capacities.

⚠️ **Get rid of defamatory content— quickly.** Faulty content is one thing. Content that falsely impugns someone's reputation is quite another. The law calls that kind of content defamatory or libelous, and you can get sued for letting it appear on your site. The disclaimer above won't protect you from liability if you're sued by someone who's been defamed on your website—in fact there's probably no language that will. If in doubt about content posted at your website, remove it immediately and consult an attorney.

2. Message Boards and Chat Rooms

Your website may have an area where users can place their own messages (a message board) or communicate with other visitors (a chat room). It's a good idea to have users agree to certain restrictions, such as the following:

MESSAGE BOARD RESTRICTIONS:

The community area of the ProtoBiz site contains a message board where you may share information with other visitors to the site. You're the only person responsible for the content and consequences of your messages. By using this site, you agree that:

You won't use the site for chain letters, spam, solicitations or bulk communications.

You won't send or post any message that is unlawful, harassing, defamatory, abusive or threatening.

You won't impersonate any other person or entity or use an inappropriate name.

ProtoBiz may delete or edit any message it decides violates its guidelines or is otherwise inappropriate.

If ProtoBiz determines that you're violating its message board guidelines, ProtoBiz may end your registration and your right to use the message board.

E. Terms for Purchasing Products

If your site sells products or services, you'll need to consider specific terms and conditions related to these transactions. And as we explain in Section G, the consumer must be able to view these terms and conditions *before* making a purchase.

1. Credit Card Use

Under federal law, a credit card user is liable only for the first $50 of unauthorized purchases provided that the user promptly notifies the credit card issuer of the unauthorized use. (15 USC § 1643.) You may want to reassure customers that they can safely use their credit cards to make purchases on your website. The following language does that and also limits your company's liability to $50 if there's a problem.

CREDIT CARD GUARANTEE

ProtoBiz wants to make shopping online a convenient and safe experience. Here's our Credit Card Guarantee:

Our computer system safeguards all payment information that you transmit to us while using our site. This includes your user name, password and credit card number and expiration date. We convert your personal information into code that is securely transmitted over the Internet.

If someone fraudulently uses your credit card information as a result of your making an online purchase from ProtoBiz, you must notify your credit card provider in accordance with its rules and procedures. If you do so, and your credit card provider holds you liable for unauthorized charges, we'll reimburse you for the liability up to $50, the limit of your liability under federal law.

2. Manufacturers' Warranties

If you sell online, you probably already offer a warranty that explains what you will and will not do for the customer if there's a problem with the product. A warranty can both reassure the customer and limit your liability. We recommend that you post your warranty at your website.

If you're an online retailer and you sell goods that carry a manufacturer's limited warranty, you may need to post warranty information, whether or not you're the manufacturer. Federal law requires that if the goods are sold for more than $15, you must tell customers how they can view the warranty before making a purchase. Consider posting a notice like this:

LIMITED WARRANTIES

Many of the products sold by ProtoBiz come with a Manufacturer's Limited Warranty. If you'd like to see the Manufacturer's Limited Warranty before you order a product, click on the warranty link, below, or email us at warranties@protobiz.com. We'll send you a copy of the warranty or tell you where you can get one.

---

3. Returns and Repairs

Your business should develop a return and repair policy, and post it on your website. For example, maybe you're prepared to give a full refund but only if the product is returned within 30 days and is in salable condition. If customers know this in advance, they won't be surprised if you refuse to give a refund 45 days after the purchase. While you have a great deal of discretion in how you decide to deal with returns and repairs, a generous policy—such as the one that follows—can build tremendous goodwill among present and prospective customers.

RETURN POLICY

We don't want you to have anything from ProtoBiz that isn't completely satisfactory. If you wish to return an item, send it to us at [address]. Enclose a note telling us:

- How you want us to handle the return. We can exchange the item, issue a gift certificate, issue a refund or credit the card originally charged.
- Why you're returning the item (for example, wrong size, damage in transit, and so on).
- The name and address to which we should send your refund or exchange.
- An email address, fax or phone number so we can contact you if we have questions.
- If you need to use freight shipping to return the item to us, call our customer service department at 800-555-1234 and we'll make the necessary arrangements.

F. Additional Terms and Conditions

Here are six more terms and conditions, some of which may be useful for your website. The first three can be used by all websites. The last three may be useful in specific situations, as explained below.

1. Jurisdiction Over Lawsuits

No business wants to be sued. Unfortunately, being sued by an Internet customer can be worse than being sued by a local customer. That's because the Internet customer will want to sue you close to home, not where you do business. If you're in Los Angeles and the customer lives on Long Island, it could be a huge expense to defend yourself. While the possibility of such a lawsuit may be remote, it helps to have your customers agree that courts in your own backyard will resolve any disputes. (See Chapter 8 for a more complete discussion of jurisdiction and issues faced by online businesses, and more strategies for avoiding out-of-state lawsuits.)

You may be able to protect yourself by saying in your postings that any disputes will be resolved in the state where your business is located. Three states (Idaho, Montana and Alabama), however, refuse to honor such jurisdiction clauses. Elsewhere, the legal rules for online jurisdiction are evolving. In a California case,

a court refused to honor America Online's jurisdiction clause. But judges in Massachusetts, Illinois, New York and Florida have ruled in favor of AOL on this same issue.

These clauses are more likely to be enforced when your business is dealing with another business than when you're dealing with a non-business consumer. Courts are sometimes reluctant to force a consumer to sue in a distant court over a $50 or $75 claim.

> **EXAMPLE:** Al Mendoza, Jr., of Sacramento, California, had a beef with America Online. He sued AOL in a California court, claiming that AOL kept charging his credit card for service even after he canceled his AOL subscription. AOL tried to have the case transferred to Virginia, citing its standard membership agreement that required all lawsuits against it to be heard there. Mendoza claimed that the agreement was part of some densely worded, small-size text that was hard to read on his computer screen. The Sacramento judge ruled that to force Mendoza to move his $65 lawsuit to Virginia would be unfair and unreasonable. (*America Online, Inc. v. The Superior Court of Alameda County,* 90 Cal. App. 4th 1 (2001).)

At any rate, having such a provision as part of your terms and conditions can do no harm. It's more likely to be enforceable if it's part of a click-through (or "click-to-accept") agreement in which the user or customer assents to your provisions.

Here's what a sample provision might look like:

JURISDICTION

The courts in Los Angeles County, California, will have exclusive jurisdiction in all disputes relating to the use of this website, and the ordering of goods and services.

---

2. Applicable Law

Since laws vary from state to state and country to country, it's best if your terms and conditions are interpreted (if a lawsuit ever arises) according to the laws of your own state. You and your lawyer will be most familiar with those laws.

To ensure this, you can specify that your state laws will apply. (The jurisdiction clause above means only that the courts in your state will have the power to decide the case—it doesn't say anything about what law they would apply.) Consider including a clause like the following one in your terms and conditions:

CHOICE OF LAW

These terms and conditions will be governed and construed in accordance with California law.

---

3. Changes in Terms and Conditions

You may want to change your terms and conditions from time to time. Visitors to your site need to know that this is a possibility. Be aware that if a customer has a dispute with you concerning a transaction, most likely the terms and conditions that were in effect at the time of the transaction will prevail. You can't expect to have new terms and conditions apply retroactively.

The following language notifies visitors that changes are possible:

ProtoBiz may change these terms and conditions with or without notice. Please review this link regularly to see any changes.

---

4. Sales Limited to USA

You may wish to limit your exposure to laws (and lawsuits) in distant places by selling only to people in the United States or even in just your home state. If you do that, you should also take reasonable steps to reject orders from people in areas beyond your targeted market. (See Chapter 8 for more on this.)

You should consider using this clause if you sell at your site, and don't want to seek legal advice on how the laws of other countries may apply to the goods or services you're selling.

If you *don't* sell goods or services at your site—for example, if your site is only an online ad—don't bother with this statement. The same is true if you only provide information or chats.

Here's a sample statement limiting sales to the United States:

SALES LIMITATION

The goods and services described on this site are available only within the United States of America.

---

5. Informational Sites

If your website is largely informational and doesn't offer goods or services for sale, you may wish to let users know early on that *using* your website means they accept your terms. It's smart to post this notice right on your home page.

Here's one type of notice you can post:

Welcome to the ProtoBiz website. Please review our terms and conditions, which govern your use of the site. By using this site, you acknowledge that you've read, understand and agree to be bound by these terms. If you don't agree to these terms, then please don't use our site.

---

6. Disclaimer for Links You Provide

If your site links to others sites of interest to your visitors, you won't want to be legally liable for anything on those sites.

EXAMPLE: Musicanna.com, a site for folk music archivists, links to music sites around the world. Musicanna is unable to police all of the linked sites to determine whether they carry infringing music. In addition, some of the linked sites contain political messages from folk musicians.

To preserve legal rights and editorial independence, consider posting a disclaimer like the following:

LINKING

This site contains links to websites operated by other businesses. ProtoBiz does not control these other sites and isn't responsible for their content. We don't necessarily endorse the linked sites or have any association with the operators of those sites.

G. How and Where to Post Your Terms and Conditions

How and where should you display your terms and conditions? At the least, you'll want to provide prominent links that easily take customers to your postings. This, by itself, provides a reasonable level of legal protection. If you want a higher degree of confidence that your terms and conditions will be binding, you'll need to add an "I Accept" button for customers to agree to your terms.

1. Links to Your Terms and Conditions

Every website needs to make sure customers can quickly find its terms and conditions through a link on the home page and other important pages, including the order page. The link can be called *Terms and Conditions* or anything else you choose that's reasonably descriptive—for example, *Our Policies, Customer Policies, Terms of Usage* or *Terms of Service*. If the link is conspicuously displayed, there's a good chance that a court would rule (if the issue ever landed in court) that visitors have accepted your terms and are bound by them. (Naturally, this assumes that your terms don't violate any law or public policy and are not grossly unfair.)

To make sure users know they can read your terms and conditions, follow these guidelines:

- Put the home page link where users can see it without having to scroll down the page.
- Put the link in large type and a distinctive color so it stands out.
- Include a link on all other pages, if possible. But at a minimum, put it

on the pages where customers place orders so they can read it first. Write your terms and conditions in plain English that people can easily understand.

- Put your terms and conditions in large type that's easy to read.

You can test your terms and conditions by asking friends to visit your site and locate and read the notices. If your friends have difficulty finding or understanding your terms, then you need to work at making the notices more prominent and more readable.

2. Requiring Actual Assent

If a dissatisfied customer sues you, you'd like the judge to treat your terms and conditions as a binding contract. Some judges will rule that if you've used conspicuous postings, it's assumed the customer read your terms and conditions and, by placing an order, is contractually bound. Other judges will say that postings are not enough. They'll find that there's a contract only if the customer specifically accepted your terms. Currently, the most practical way to do this is to present your terms to your customers, and then require them to click a button at the end that says "I accept" or "I agree" before they can complete the transaction.

This way, if a dispute ever goes to court, you'll have evidence that the customer not only was given the chance to read your terms and conditions by clicking a link, but agreed to them. For example, when a group of consumers sued Netscape over software they'd downloaded from the Netscape website, the company tried to get the case kicked out of court because the posted terms of use required arbitration of such disputes. The judge refused because visitors hadn't been required to indicate their assent to the arbitration clause. (*Specht v. Netscape Communications Corp.*, 150 F. Supp. 2d 585 (S.D. N.Y. 2001)).

Most websites don't require customers to click an "I accept" button, probably because this complicates and slows down the ordering process, which could result in a lost sale from an impatient customer.

In some cases, you may want to want to screen out visitors before they can use parts of your site. For example, if your site offers information, you can require visitors to click their acceptance before they can reach the site's key features. This might appeal to you if your site dispenses information about legal or medical matters. In that case, you can link to your terms and conditions from your home page (or nearby) and require visitors to accept them before they can proceed deeper into your site.

Keep an Eye on E-Signature Technology

If someone accepts your terms and conditions by clicking "I accept," how do you know who that someone is? You usually won't know for sure. That can be a problem if there's ever a dispute in court, because you'll probably need to prove that the customer—not a spouse, a child, a stranger or the family dog—was really the one who accepted your terms.

Apparently, this issue hasn't surfaced yet in real-world litigation—at least not in published court decisions. Fortunately, technology is being developed which will allow customers to digitally sign contracts over the Internet. The signature may not be a traditional signature. The process that gains acceptance may involve a device that scans the customer's retina or fingerprints. Or perhaps a device will read a coded plastic card—in which case the customer will also enter a personal identification number like the ones used at ATM machines. Whatever the process, when the technology is available and widely used, it will be easy to identify the person you're dealing with in cyberspace.

Congress anticipated the emergence of digital-signature technology when it enacted the Electronic Signature in Global and National Commerce Act (E-Sign for short). This law acknowledges that electronic contracts and signatures have the same legal status as those consisting of paper and ink.

Working With Other Websites

ometimes, one plus one can add up to more than two. A great way to get more mileage from your website—such as attracting more visitors—is to join forces with other websites. Arrangements between websites take many forms and go by many names, including joint marketing, co-branding, cooperative marketing and strategic alliances. But whatever the name of your team efforts, the resulting synergy can turbocharge your site, making it more likely that you'll be successful. Most e-commerce alliances are built on one or two strategies:

- *Content Sharing.* One company gives its content to another, to use on the other's site. Or the companies may trade content.

- *Sales and Referrals.* A company arranges to sell its products or services (or get referrals) on another company's site. Again, there may be cross-selling or cross-referrals.

Each strategy offers possibilities for both companies to profit. For example, companies that share content can divvy up ad revenue from pages with shared content. A company that sells another's products or services can receive a commission from those sales; the company that produces the goods or services, of course, profits from the increased sales.

This chapter describes some ways that your online business can join forces with other online businesses. It also covers the legal issues raised by these arrangements and explains how you can create legal agreements that address them.

In this chapter, you'll find the following forms that you can adapt to your situation:

- **Linking Agreement.** Allows a site to display another business's trademarks, copyrights or other protected material if it links to the owner's site. See Section A.

- **Affiliate Agreement.** Lets one site sell or promote the products or services of another and earn a commission for each sale generated. See Section B.

- **Content Licensing Agreement.** Gives an e-business permission to use content owned by another business in return for a fee, revenue from online sales or advertising, or other compensation. See Section C.

Each agreement is unique, and we recommend that you modify each as necessary to suit your needs. If you use simple, unambiguous language, your agreement will be understandable and enforceable. Avoid legal-sounding gobbledygook such as "heretofore" and "therein."

A. A Simple Linking Agreement

Typically, linking to another site isn't the subject of major negotiations. The site that's being linked to usually is happy to get the exposure and won't object—although it might do so if it feels that the site linking to it is offensive or otherwise unacceptable. Still, linking to another site without permission may result in a conflict, so it generally makes sense to ask permission via a short emailed note. For example, a statement such as:

> TO: BUSINESS MANAGER/
> OFFICESUPPLIESTOYOURDOOR.COM
>
> I'm the webmaster for protobiz.com, a small business site. We're providing links from our site to small business resources. We'd like to create a hypertext link to officesuppliestoyourdoor.com. Please let me know if that's acceptable.
>
> Jim@protobiz.com

If your link will use anyone else's trademarked or copyrighted material, it's a good idea to use the linking agreement we provide below. Our linking agreement gives the linking site (the Source Site) permission to use the trademarked, copyrighted or other protected material owned by the site being linked to (the Destination Site) for the purposes of the link itself. For instance, when a site offers a link such as "Click to the Microsoft site," it's using a trademark of the Microsoft company, which Microsoft can prevent others from using.

Linking Agreement

1. Names

This Agreement is made by _____ (Source Site) and
_____ (Destination Site).

Explanation: *For recommended ways to enter names in a contract, see Chapter 3, Section F.*

2. The Link

Source Site will provide a link to Destination Site's website. The link will appear on the Source Site at the following URL: _____

The Link will appear as follows: _____

❏ The text at the Source Site that includes the link to the Destination Site website will read as follows: _____

with the words _____ highlighted and underlined to make the actual Hypertext link.

❏ An image link described as follows: _____.

The Link will take users to the following URL at the Destination Site: _____.

The Link to the Destination URL, or to any other page at the Destination Site, will not be framed.

Explanation: *Enter the URL of the Source Site page where the link will appear. Next, check one or both of the options for how the link will appear: a text link, an image link or both. For the options you choose, fill in the required information, including the sentence in which the link will appear, the actual words that make up the link and a description of the image, depending on what type of link you'll use. Next, enter the URL at the Destination Site where the link will connect.*

Our agreement prohibits framing, which is a method of linking that loads the information from the Destination Site into a window at the Source Site, rather than simply going to the Destination Site. Most sites don't like to be framed, and would rather have a regular link to their site. If you don't want to prohibit framed links, you can remove this language.

3. Grant of Rights

Destination Site grants to Source Site the nonexclusive rights, including all trademark, copyright and other intellectual property rights, to display the Link at the Source Site website, if the specifications of Section 2 of this Agreement are met and if Source Site maintains the integrity of the Link. Destination Site reserves the right to revoke this Grant of Rights.

Explanation: *This section allows the Source Site to use protected intellectual property of the Destination Site such as trademarked or copyrighted information for purposes of the link. It also establishes that the Destination Site may revoke permission.*

4. Standards and Notices

Source Site will maintain its website in accordance with industry standards. Upon notice from Destination Site, Source Site will promptly remove the Link if requested. Source Site will promptly notify Destination Site of any changes to the Link or to the Source Site affecting the Link.

Explanation: *This clause requires the Source Site to maintain its site to reasonable standards, remove the link upon notice from the Destination Site and notify the Destination Site of any changes to the link or the Source Site that will affect the link.*

Dated: _____

SOURCE SITE:

Name of Business:

_____

A _____

By: _____

Printed Name and Title: _____

Address: _____

DESTINATION SITE:

Name of Business:

_____

A _____

By: _____

Printed Name and Title: _____

Address: _____

Explanation: *Follow the instructions for signing found in Chapter 3, Section F4.*

B. Sales and Referrals

Almost every really good website links to other sites. Users expect and value this connectivity, and your business can serve your customers and increase revenue by taking advantage of it wisely.

> **EXAMPLE:** ProtoBiz creates prototypes of inventions. In addition to advertising its services, ProtoBiz.com's website lists popular design books and software products. Since it lacks the ability to provide a shopping cart at its site—and doesn't want to be in the book and software business— ProtoBiz creates an alliance with a bookstore site and links to the site for sales of books and software. In return, ProtoBiz earns a commission on each sale.

1. Creating Affiliate Relationships

If you link to other sites, you may be able to earn a commission for the sales you generate by the traffic you send to those sites. And if other sites link to yours, you get more traffic, more sales, and possibly greater prominence in search engine results (some search engines, notably google.com, rank sites by how many other sites link to them). These arrange-ments are typically called *affiliate* relationships. Most large online retailers have affiliate programs and you can learn about them by clicking the appropriate link on the site's home page. In the case of smaller business, just email if you want to inquire about alliances.

2. The Affiliate Agreement

It's essential to capture your affiliate relationship in an agreement, and we provide one here along with instructions. An agreement like this one is appropriate whether you're the site that owns and sells the goods (the E-Retailer) or the site that refers the sales to that site (the Affiliate).

Affiliate Agreement

1. Names

This Agreement is made by _____ (E-Retailer) and
_____ (Affiliate).

Explanation: *Enter the name of each party. For information on the proper way to deal with names in a contract, see Chapter 3, Section F.*

2. Definitions

Intellectual Property Rights are all rights in and to trade secrets, patents, copyrights and trademarks, as well as moral rights and similar rights under domestic or foreign law.

Net Sales means the aggregate amount actually paid to E-Retailer for Qualified Purchases, excluding sales taxes, shipping, handling and other similar charges, amounts due to credit card fraud and bad debt and credits for returned goods.

E-Retailer Brand Features are any trademarks, service marks, logos and other distinctive Brand Features of E-Retailer that are used in or relate to the E-Retailer, including the trademarks, service marks and logos described in Attachment A.

Qualified Purchases are purchases of E-Retailer products made by Affiliate site users. Qualified Purchases are those that (a) are purchased by users of the E-Retailer site who come directly from the Affiliate site via hyperlinked GIFs or associated text links, (b) are sold by E-Retailer and shipped by E-Retailer and (c) for which E-Retailer has received full payment.

Explanation: *This section defines terms that will be used repeatedly in the agreement.*

3. Recitals

3.1 *E-Retailer.* E-Retailer _____.

3.2 *Affiliate.* Affiliate is the operator of the website _____.

3.3 *Commission.* Affiliate's site will generate sales of E-Retailer products and Affiliate will receive a commission on Qualified Purchases of those products.

Explanation: *This section sets out background information and the nature of the affiliate agreement. First, describe the E-Retailer's business, making sure to identify the types of sales that will be part of the affiliate agreement. Also enter the address (URL) of the Affiliate's website.*

EXAMPLE:

3.1 *E-Retailer*. E-Retailer operates an online business selling houseware and kitchenware.

3.2 *Affiliate*. Affiliate is the operator of the website www.coolstuff.com.

3.3 *Commission*. Affiliate's site will generate sales of E-Retailer products and Affiliate will receive a commission on Qualified Purchases of those products.

4. Terms

4.1 *Non-Exclusivity*. This is a non-exclusive Agreement. Both E-Retailer and Affiliate are free to form affiliations with other sites.

4.2 *Links*. Affiliate agrees to prominently display hyperlinked graphical images (hyperlinked GIFs), with dimensions of no less than _____ pixels, of the following E-Retailer products: _____. Affiliate agrees to co-operate with E-Retailer in establishing and maintaining these graphical image links.

4.3 *Brand Features*. E-Retailer grants a non-exclusive, worldwide, fully paid license to use, reproduce and display the E-Retailer Brand Features on the Affiliate's site.

Explanation: *This section provides that the agreement is non-exclusive, which means that the E-Retailer is free to sign similar agreements with other affiliates, and the Affiliate is free to promote products of other e-retailers. It also requires the Affiliate to display graphic links (hyperlinked GIFs) to the E-Retailer site, and specifies that the graphic links be of a certain size. Thumbnail images on Web pages tend to be in the 20 by 20 pixel range. Enter whatever dimensions you and the other party have agreed on. Also enter the products that the Affiliate agrees to display.*

Since the graphic links are likely trademarks owned by the E-Retailer, this section also grants permission to the Affiliate to display them at its site. The agreement uses the term "brand features" to refer to trademarks and logos of the E-Retailer, as defined in the definitions section.

5. Commissions

5.1 The commission rate on all E-Retailer products will be ____% of Net Sales for Qualified Purchases. Commissions will be paid to Affiliate ____ monthly ____ quarterly and mailed with a detailed Sales Report for that period. Payments will be sent to Affiliate within ____ days following the end of each ____ month ____ quarter.

5.2 Affiliate is eligible to earn commissions only on sales occurring during the term outlined in Section 8.1 and 8.2 of this agreement. Commissions earned through the date of termination will remain payable only if the related E-Retailer product orders are not canceled or returned. E-Retailer may withhold the Affiliate's final payment for a reasonable time to ensure that the correct amount is paid.

Explanation: *Enter the commission percentage that you and the other party have agreed upon. Many affiliate agreements have a commission of 5% or 10% of net sales. Then choose whether payments will be sent monthly or quarterly, and state how many days after the end of the month or quarter the payments will be due (usually 30, 60 or 90 days).*

6. Customer Relations and Policies

All customers who buy products from E-Retailer are considered to be customers of E-Retailer. All E-Retailer rules, policies and operating procedures concerning customer orders, customer service and E-Retailer product sales will apply to these customers. E-Retailer reserves the right to change its products, prices, policies and operating procedures at any time. E-Retailer will use commercially reasonable efforts to provide Affiliate with accurate product information, but cannot guarantee the availability or price of any particular product.

Explanation: *This section establishes that the customer relations, pricing and other service policies of the E-Retailer (not the Affiliate) apply to the transactions, which can be changed at the E-Retailer's discretion. The clause also requires the E-Retailer to give correct product or service information to the Affiliate.*

7. Records, Sales Reports and Audits

Both parties will maintain accurate records with respect to the calculation of all payments due under this Agreement. E-Retailer will provide Affiliate with monthly Sales Reports, by the _____day of each month.

Once each year, Affiliate will have the right, upon at least _____days' prior written notice to E-Retailer, to appoint an independent third party to audit E-Retailer's books and records reasonably related to the calculation of such payments to verify compliance with the terms of this Agreement. Any such audit will take place during E-Retailer's regular business hours and will be conducted in a manner that does not unreasonably interfere with E-Retailer's business activities. Such audit will be at Affiliate's expense; however, if the audit reveals overdue payments in excess of_____% of the payments owed to date, E-Retailer will immediately pay the cost of such audit, and Affiliate may conduct another audit during the same one-year period.

Explanation: *In the Records, Sales Reports and Audits section, enter which day of the month the E-Retailer must provide sales reports to the other website. Choose whatever day you want.*

Next, enter the number of days' notice that will be required for the Affiliate to inspect the sales records of the E-Retailer. Then enter what percentage of underpayment will trigger a penalty; 5% or 10% percent is typical.

8. Term and Termination

8.1 *Initial Term*. This Agreement takes effect on _____ (the Effective Date). Unless the Agreement is sooner terminated as provided below, it will remain effective for an Initial Term of ____ months following the Effective Date.

8.2 *Renewal*. After the Initial Term, this Agreement will be automatically renewed for successive additional ____-month periods (Extension Terms). Either party, however, may prevent a renewal from taking effect by notifying the other party at least 60 days before the end of the Initial Term or an Extension Term.

8.3 *Performance Prevented*. If a party cannot perform any of its obligations due to a cause beyond the reasonable control of the party, that party's performance will be excused and the time for performance will be extended for the period of delay or inability to perform due to such occurrence.

8.4 *Termination*. Either party may terminate this Agreement if the other party:

(a) fails to make timely payments as provided in this Agreement and such failure is not remedied within 30 days after written notice to such party, or

(b) breaches any material obligations under this Agreement and the breach is not remedied within 30 days after written notice to such party.

8.5 *Effect of Termination*. Unless terminated for cause, any termination under this Section 8 will be without any liability or obligation of the terminating party. The provisions of Sections 8, 10, 11 and 12 will survive termination of this Agreement.

Explanation: *Another important matter to cover is how long the agreement will last. This is known as the term. Typically, an affiliate agreement has an initial term, say for one year, and then may be automatically renewed, say for six months at a time.*

Bundled with the provisions for the term of the agreement are provisions for ending the agreement. Generally, an agreement can be terminated either by choice of one or both of the parties, or for cause—for example, if one party doesn't make required payments or makes unauthorized use of the content.

This agreement provides for automatic renewal but allows either party to terminate by giving notice at least 60 days before the end of the current term.

The "Termination for Cause" provision (8.4) sets out certain circumstances in which either party may terminate the contract. It also allows a party to correct a breach within 30 days. If you don't want to allow that, remove the language that allows it.

The "survival" provision establishes that even though the agreement between the parties is over, certain obligations—for example, indemnification, limitation of liability and the right to make ownership claims—will continue.

9.   Advertising Revenue Sharing

The parties agree to the Advertising Revenue Sharing terms in Attachment B.

Explanation: It's possible that the Affiliate may sell advertising on pages that feature the E-Retailer's products. If the E-Retailer's products are featured prominently enough on the page or could be said to be the primary draw to the page, the E-Retailer may demand a share of revenues from any ads on the page. If you and the other party want this kind of arrangement, check the box and enter the details of your arrangement in an attachment called Attachment B.

10. Indemnification

Affiliate, at its own expense, will indemnify, defend and hold harmless E-Retailer, its affiliates and their employees, directors, agents and affiliates, against any third-party claim, suit, action or other proceeding brought against E-Retailer, to the extent that it is based on or arises from any unauthorized use of any E-Retailer Brand Features made by Affiliate. Affiliate will pay any and all costs, damages and expenses, including reasonable attorneys' fees and costs awarded against or otherwise incurred by E-Retailer in connection with or arising from any such third-party claim, suit, action or proceeding.

E-Retailer, at its own expense, will indemnify, defend and hold harmless Affiliate, its employees, directors, agents and affiliates, against any third-party claim, suit, action or other proceeding brought against Affiliate based on or arising from a claim that a E-Retailer Brand Feature infringes in any manner any intellectual property right of any third party or contains any material or information that is obscene, defamatory, libelous, slanderous, that violates any third party's right of publicity, privacy or personality, or has otherwise resulted in any tort, injury, violation of applicable law or regulation, damage or harm to any person.

Explanation: These indemnity provisions protect each party from liability arising from certain lawsuits. Generally, when a party indemnifies another party, it agrees to protect the other party from damages and legal fees in specified cases.

Indemnification can be risky and expensive, so parties often resist these clauses. However, it's also important for new business allies to feel safe and protected when entering into agreements. Whether you or the other party will be able to insist on an indemnity provision will depend on your bargaining power.

11. Limitation of Liability

NEITHER E-RETAILER NOR AFFILIATE WILL BE LIABLE TO THE OTHER PARTY FOR IN-DIRECT, INCIDENTAL, CONSEQUENTIAL, SPECIAL OR EXEMPLARY DAMAGES ARISING FROM THIS AGREEMENT, EVEN IF THAT PARTY HAS BEEN ADVISED OF THE POSSIBIL-ITY OF SUCH DAMAGES, INCLUDING LOSS OF REVENUE OR ANTICIPATED PROFITS OR LOST BUSINESS.

Explanation: *This section deals with what happens if one party sues the other for breach of contract. It limits the liability of each party to monetary losses actually suffered. Neither party will be entitled to other damages that might be available under state law. In other words, if one party successfully sues for breach of contract, the winner will be entitled only to its actual losses, such as any amounts it was underpaid. It won't be able to claim or recover other damages—for example, punitive damages intended to punish the breaching party.*

12. Ownership

Affiliate acknowledges and agrees that:

12.1 E-Retailer owns all right, title and interest in the E-Retailer Brand Features.

12.2 Nothing in this Agreement confers in Affiliate any right of ownership in the E-Retailer Brand Features.

12.3 Affiliate will not contest the validity of the E-Retailer Brand Features.

12.4 No licenses are granted by either party except for those set forth in this Agreement.

Explanation: *The ownership section establishes the ownership rights of each party, making it totally clear who owns the brand features.*

13. Public Announcements

The parties will cooperate to create appropriate public announcements relating to the relationship set forth in this Agreement. Neither party will make any public announcement regarding the existence or content of this Agreement without the other party's prior written approval.

Explanation: *This section provides that neither party will announce the deal to the public without the other party's written approval. It also states that the parties agree to work together in planning and creating any public announcements about the arrangement.*

14. Disputes

(Choose One)

❏ Mediation. If a dispute arises, the parties will try in good faith to settle it through mediation conducted by: _____

❏ a mediator to be mutually selected.

The parties will share the costs of the mediator equally. Each party will cooperate fully and fairly with the mediator and will attempt to reach a mutually satisfactory resolution to the dispute. If the dispute is not resolved within 30 days after it is referred to the mediator, either party may take the matter to court.

❏ Mediation and Possible Arbitration. If a dispute arises, the parties will try in good faith to settle it through mediation conducted by: _____

❏ a mediator to be mutually selected.

The parties will share the costs of the mediator equally. Each party will cooperate fully and fairly with the mediator and will attempt to reach a mutually satisfactory solution to the dispute. If the dispute is not resolved within 30 days after it is referred to the mediator, it will be arbitrated by: _____

❏ an arbitrator to be mutually selected.

Judgment on the arbitration award may be entered in any court that has jurisdiction over the matter. The arbitrator will allocate costs of arbitration, including attorney fees.

Explanation: *Provisions 14 through 23, which are standard in most contracts, are explained in Chapter 3, Section F.*

15. Relationships

This Agreement does not make either party a partner, joint venturer or employee of the other party.

16. Invalid Provisions

If a court finds any provision of this Agreement invalid or unenforceable, the remainder of this Agreement will be interpreted so as best to carry out the parties' intent.

17. Entire Agreement

This is the entire Agreement between the parties. It replaces and supersedes any oral agreements between the parties, as well as any prior writings.

18. Modification

Any modifications to this Agreement must be in writing.

19. Waiver

The failure to exercise any right in this Agreement will not waive prior or subsequent rights.

20. Notices

All notices must be in writing. A notice may be delivered to a party at the address the party designates in writing. A notice may be delivered:

(a) in person

(b) by certified mail, or

(c) by overnight courier.

21. Successors and Assigns

This agreement binds and benefits the heirs, successors and assigns of the parties.

22. Attorney Fees and Expenses

If there is litigation, the prevailing party may collect from the other party its reasonable costs and attorney fees incurred in enforcing this Agreement.

23. Governing Law

This Agreement will be governed by and construed in accordance with the laws of the state of _____.

Dated: _____

E-RETAILER:

Name of Business:

_____

A _____

By:_____

Printed Name and Title: _____

Address: _____

AFFILIATE:

Name of Business:

_____

A _____

By:_____

Printed Name and Title: _____

Address: _____

Explanation: *Follow the instructions for signing in Chapter 3, Section F4.*

Attachment A
E-Retailer Brand Features

E-Retailer business name:_____

Related logos: _____

[Optional] Attachment B
Advertising Revenue Sharing

1. Definitions

Net Advertising Revenue means all revenue from advertising and sponsorships that appear on Product Pages.

2. Agreement to Share Advertising Revenue

2.1 *Commissions.* Affiliate will pay E-Retailer ____% of the Net Advertising Revenue that accrues to Affiliate during the term of this Agreement from advertising and sponsorships that appear on Content Pages.

2.2 *Payments.* Payments by Affiliate to E-Retailer will be made monthly within 30 days of the end of each calendar month. With each payment, Affiliate will provide to E-Retailer documentation reasonably detailing the calculation of the payment.

2.3 *Responsibility for Selling Advertising.* Affiliate will be solely responsible for selling any advertising on the Affiliate Site.

3. Audits and Reports

3.1 *Records and Inspections.* Affiliate will maintain accurate records with respect to the calculation of all payments due under this Agreement. E-Retailer and its representative may, upon at least 30 days' prior written notice to Affiliate, and no more than once a year, inspect Affiliate records reasonably related to the calculation of such payments. Inspections will take place during Affiliate's normal business hours. If an inspection reveals any underpayment of fees by Affiliate of greater than 5%, Affiliate will promptly reimburse E-Retailer for all costs of the audit along with the amount due.

3.2 *Usage Reports.* Affiliate will send E-Retailer, via email, usage reports containing the total number of page views generated by Content Pages. Each usage report will cover a calendar month and will be delivered within 15 days following the end of the applicable month.

4. Competitor Advertising

4.1 Affiliate will not sell, allow to be sold, post or allow to be posted on Content Pages any advertising of the following Competitors of E-Retailer:

4.2 Upon ____ days' written notice to Affiliate, E-Retailer may expand the list of Competitors to reflect any ventures that E-Retailer was unaware of when this Agreement was signed.

Explanation: *If you won't be sharing advertising revenues, then don't include this attachment.*

If you are going to share ad revenues, this attachment will contain the details of your arrangement. Enter the commission percentage—that is, the percentage of any revenue from advertising that appears on pages with licensed content—that the Affiliate will pay the E-Retailer. A rate of 50% of net advertising revenue is common, though it will depend on the bargaining power of the parties (as always) and how valuable the content is.

E-Retailers typically want to make sure that the Affiliate keeps good track of advertising revenues to ensure that the payments being made are fair and accurate. It's good practice to require the Affiliate to keep adequate records, and to give the content owner the right to occasionally inspect those records after giving adequate notice.

An E-Retailer obviously won't want an Affiliate to permit any competitor to advertise on pages of licensed content. It's a good idea to include a provision that prohibits competitor advertising in the ad revenue sharing terms. A prohibition on competitor advertising can refer to a list of known competitors, which the content owner may update periodically as new competitors may enter the market. In the Competitor Advertising section, enter the number of days' notice that will be required for the licensor to add to the list of competitors. A 30-day notice period is generally adequate and typical.

C. Sharing Content

You may want to use some content from another website, or another website may want to use some of yours. This section explains how you can profit by sharing content, and show you how to create a content-sharing agreement.

1. Benefits of Sharing Content

Sharing content can offer several benefits: increased exposure for your business, more sales, and revenue from advertising.

a. Increased Exposure and Traffic

Few small businesses can expect to make much money by letting others use their content. But permitting someone else to use it (with or without a fee) can help your website content reach as wide an audience as possible.

Even better, you can require the site that's using your content to include prominent links back to your website. With linking, not only does your content get increased exposure, but so does your website.

b. Advertising Revenue

A site that pays to use someone else's content generally does so to make the site more attractive to potential visitors—and to advertisers. The more desirable or high-profile the content—for example, mutual fund reviews by a nationally recognized expert, or CD reviews from *Rolling Stone*—the more it will draw advertisers.

If a site sells advertising on pages with licensed content, the content owner will typically want to receive either a portion of the ad revenue, a flat license fee or both.

c.   Increased Sales

If you have content that's related to the products or services you sell online, and you license it to another website, you can increase your sales by requiring the licensee to include product information and a link back to your website. Let's say, for instance, an outdoor equipment company licenses an article about rock climbing to a travel website. The equipment company may require the travel site to include on the article page a small thumbnail picture of rock climbing gear and a link to the sales area of the equipment company's website. This not only creates a direct sales opportunity for the outdoors company, but also potential profits for the travel site which may receive a commission on sales generated from its site.

2.   Structuring a Content-Sharing Arrangement

Whether you're providing content or paying for it, you and the other party need to reach clear agreement on each other's rights and responsibilities. You need to spell out exactly what content is being licensed, how it can be used and for how long. In addition, you should agree on any special issues that are part of your deal, such as sharing ad revenue. These key issues are discussed below.

Many types of content sharing deals are possible. Don't limit yourself to the arrangements described in this chapter. Be innovative. You may be able to negotiate something much different. If you're creative and you enjoy doing deals, there's almost no limit to what you might come up with.

a.   How the Content Will Be Used

Just because a content owner gives a business permission to use its content doesn't mean that the business can do whatever it wants with the material. Content licenses grant permission for a specific set of allowable uses, which should be spelled out in the agreement. If the content will simply appear on certain pages of the website, say so explicitly. If the content will also be used in other ways—for instance, in an interactive directory or in a downloadable product—make sure the agreement reflects it. Also, specify anything that's not allowed, such as posting a file in Adobe's Portable Document Format (PDF) or making a file downloadable.

b. Branding and Links

Since a major benefit of licensing content to others is gaining increased exposure, it's usually important for the content owner to make sure information about its company or website appears with the licensed content. This might include the name of the content owner's business, its website address, its logo and other appropriate information. Making sure the company name and logo are included and distributed with the content is generally referred to as "branding," because it promotes the brand name of the content owner. On the Web, branding generally involves transforming the company name or logo into a hypertext link back to the content owner's page.

A license agreement should specify what branding or links must accompany the licensed content. It should also identify any other information required on the site—for example disclaimers regarding any advice or proprietary copyright and trademark notices—and how and where that information will appear.

c. Sharing Revenue From Advertising

If a website sells advertising on the pages that contain licensed content, the content owner will generally require that it receive a portion of the ad revenues. If so, the content license should say how the ad revenue will be shared. Depending on how lengthy the terms are, these provisions may be included in the contract, or attached to it as an "attachment."

d. Sharing Revenue From E-Commerce

A content owner and a website that licenses that content can share revenues generated from online sales of products or services. For instance, a content owner might require the website to link back to the content owner's site where related products are sold. In turn, the other website may receive a commission for its role in generating sales. Any such arrangement should be detailed in the content license.

It's important to define which sales qualify for the commission. Most e-commerce revenue sharing agreements define "qualified sales" as purchases made by users who arrived via a link from the referring site. In addition, it's common to define qualified sales as those actually purchased from and shipped by the sales site, and for which full payment has been made.

3. A Content License Agreement

When you're ready to put together your agreement, go through our form and its instructions. Most of the items to fill in and the right boxes to check are fairly self-explanatory. Several terms in this agreement are similar to those in the Affiliate Agreement (Section B, above). When appropriate, we refer you to the instructions in that section rather than repeat them here.

Content License Agreement

1. Names

This Agreement is made by _____ (Licensor) and
_____ (Licensee).

Explanation: *Fill in the name of the company that owns the content (the Licensor) and the company that will have permission to use the content (the Licensee). For instructions on filling in names in contracts, see Chapter 3, Section F4.*

2. Definitions

Content Pages are pages on Licensee's website on which Licensed Content makes up a substantial portion of the content.

Intellectual Property Rights are all rights to trade secrets, patents, copyrights and trademarks as well as moral rights and similar rights under domestic or foreign law.

Licensee Brand Features are trademarks, service marks, logos and other distinctive brand features of Licensee that are used by or relate to Licensee, including the trademarks, service marks and logos described in Attachment A.

Licensor Brand Features are all trademarks, service marks, logos and other distinctive brand features of Licensor that are used in or relate to the Licensed Content, including the trademarks, service marks and logos described in Attachment A.

Licensed Content is all materials, data and similar information collected and owned by Licensor, as described in Attachment A, that the Licensee will use subject to the terms of this Agreement, including any modifications or enhancements provided by Licensor.

Explanation: *This section defines terms that are repeatedly used in the agreement.*

3. Grant of Rights

3.1 *Content License.* Licensor grants to Licensee the following license for the Licensed Content: the _ exclusive _ non-exclusive worldwide right to reproduce, display, distribute and transmit _ and modify the Licensed Content in electronic form via the Internet and World Wide Web at Licensee's website _____ and

❐ via proprietary networks such as America Online or MSN

❐ via telephone and wireless networks.

3.2 *Brand License.* Licensor grants to Licensee the following license for the Licensor Brand

Features: The non-exclusive worldwide right to use, reproduce, display, distribute and transmit the Licensor Brand Features in connection with the presentation of the Licensed Content on Content Pages, and in connection with the marketing and promotion of Licensee.

3.3 *Limitations on License.* Licensee will not distribute the Licensed Content via any protocol other than HTTP _ or SMTP _ or FTP.

In addition:

❒ Licensee may modify the Licensed Content only as necessary to fit the format and look and feel of the Licensee Internet Site.

❒ Hypertext links provided as part of Licensed Content will not be modified or removed without Licensor's prior written approval.

❒ Licensee will not reformat the Licensed Content into PDF documents or any other downloadable format.

Licensor reserves all rights other than those conveyed or granted in this Agreement.

3.4 *Sublicensing.*

❒ Licensee may sublicense the Licensed Content.

❒ Licensee may not sublicense the Licensed Content without prior written approval of Licensor.

3.5 *Notices.* Licensee will not alter or impair any acknowledgment of copyright or other Intellectual Property Rights of Licensor that may appear in the Licensed Content and the Licensor Brand Features. This includes all copyright, trademark and similar notices that Licensor may reasonably request.

3.6 *Branding and Links.* The parties will maintain the Branding and hypertext links specified in Attachment C.

Explanation: *It may seem obvious, but you must nail down exactly what content is being licensed. The content can be described on a separate page attached to the agreement as Attachment A (Licensed Content), which we explain below.*

Also specify what rights are being granted to the licensee, such as:

- *whether the right to use the content is exclusive or non-exclusive*
- *the specific rights being granted, such as the right to reproduce, distribute, display, modify and so on—and any limitations on those rights*
- *the allowed uses for the licensed content—for example, sublicensing, and*
- *the notices required for the content and branding.*

Let's look at each of these in more detail.

a. Exclusive vs. Non-Exclusive Rights

Most online content licenses are non-exclusive. This means that the content owner can give permission to other parties to use the same content. By contrast, when exclusive rights are granted, no one else may use that material in the same way.

If exclusive rights being granted, it's crucial that you insert details about what "exclusive" really means to you. For instance, if a content provider grants an exclusive license to a website to "publish" a series of gardening columns owned by the content provider, can the content provider also grant a license to a television network to create a TV series based on the gardening columns? Since the television network isn't exactly "publishing" the gardening columns, the content owner might argue that this doesn't violate the exclusive right to "publish" the columns.

On the form, check a box to indicate whether the agreement is non-exclusive or exclusive.

Enter the website address where the licensee may post the content. Also, check the appropriate boxes if the licensee is allowed to distribute the content on other networks—for example, to set up a special site within America Online or transmit the content over wireless networks such as Sprint.

b. Territory

The territory of a content license agreement is the geographical area in which rights are being granted, such as "United States," "U.S. and Canada" or "worldwide." Since the content is for posting on a website, then the territory should be "worldwide" to reflect the fact that the content will be available all over the globe.

c. Specific Rights Being Granted

When a company owns the copyright to an article or other material, it owns the right to reproduce, distribute, sell, modify and display that article. (Copyright is discussed in detail in Chapter 5.) Any or all of these rights can be granted to someone else through a content license, so it's important that the license identify exactly which ones are included in the agreement.

Typically, a website obtains the rights to display, reproduce, distribute and transmit the content. Licensees may also be given the right to modify the content, subject to certain limits. Licensees are commonly allowed to modify content only to make it fit the look and feel of the licensee's website. Or, a licensor may grant a slightly broader right to modify the content, such as the right to divide it into sections or to modify section headers. Another common limitation on the right to modify is to forbid the removal of any hypertext links contained in the content.

d. Limitations on Rights

It's common for a content license to state that any rights not explicitly granted to the licensee are reserved by the content owner. This is sometimes called a reservation of rights clause. It means that the rights being conveyed to the licensee include only what's stated in the agreement and nothing more.

Check the appropriate boxes if the licensee is allowed to distribute the content via email (SMTP) or File Transfer Protocol (FTP). Also check the appropriate boxes for limitations on the licensee's rights.

e. Sublicensing

The content license should state whether or not the licensee is free to sublicense the content—in other words, license it to a third party. Allowing sublicensing may be fine in some situations, but many content owners prefer to keep tighter control on their content and don't allow it without their written permission. Check the appropriate box.

f. Notices

If you own content and trademarks, you should include proprietary notices such as © to signify copyright or TM or ® to signify trademark ownership. In Chapter 6, Section C, we explain the significance of these notices.

Content License Agreement, *continued*

4. Fees and Delivery of Licensed Content

4.1 *Content Licensing Fees.*

❏ Licensee will pay Licensor the fees listed in Attachment B.

❏ License fees are waived.

4.2 *Delivery of Content.*

❏ Licensor will deliver the Licensed Content to Licensee within _____ days after Licensee pays the license fee.

❏ Licensor will deliver the Licensed Content to Licensee by _____.

Explanation: *If a fee will be charged for the content itself—apart from any revenue-sharing deals that we'll discuss below—check the first box. If no fees will be charged, check the second box.*

Enter the number of days that the licensor will have to deliver the content after the licensee pays the license fee. Ten or 20 days is common. If no fee is charged, just enter the agreed-upon effective date.

5. Maintenance of Licensed Content

5.1 *Licensee's Responsibilities.* In addition to any responsibilities that may be listed in Attachment D, Licensee is responsible for the design, layout, posting and maintenance of the Content Pages. Licensee is under no obligation to post any of the Licensed Content on its website.

5.2 *Licensor Assistance.* In addition to any responsibilities that may be listed in Attachment D, and upon Licensee's request, Licensor will provide, without charge, reasonable assistance to Licensee with regard to technical and service-oriented issues relating to the Licensed Content. If the content is of a factual or timely nature, Licensor will use commercially reasonable efforts to ensure that the Licensed Content is accurate and updated regularly as set forth in Attachment D.

5.3 *Updates.* Licensor will deliver any updates of the Licensed Content to Licensee in accordance with Attachment D. Licensor will give Licensee reasonable advance notice of any significant enhancements of the Licensed Content, and will make such enhancements available to Licensee upon commercially reasonable terms.

Explanation: *This establishes that the licensee is responsible for designing, laying out and maintaining the content at its site, and also says that the licensee isn't obligated to actually post the content. It goes on to state that the licensor must help the licensee with technical and service-oriented issues regarding the content, such as formatting or compatibility problems. It also requires the licensor to keep any factual or time-sensitive content up to date as much as is commercially reasonable, and to notify the licensee if it makes significant enhancements to the content. These provisions are further detailed in Attachment D, "Delivery and Technical Specifications."*

❏ 6. Advertising Revenue Sharing

The parties agree to the Advertising Revenue Sharing terms in Attachment E.

Explanation: *This optional section establishes that the parties will share revenues from advertising on content pages, and refers to Attachment E, "Advertising Revenue Sharing," for the details. If you and the other party won't be sharing advertising revenue, then don't check the box. If you will be sharing advertising revenues, then do check the box and enter the details of your agreement in Attachment E, explained below.*

❏ 7. E-Commerce Revenue Sharing

The parties agree to the E-Commerce Revenue Sharing terms in Attachment F.

Explanation: *This optional section establishes that the licensor and licensee will share revenues from sales generated at the licensee's site, and refers to Attachment F, "E-Commerce Revenue Sharing," for the details. If you and the other party have no plans for sharing revenues from online sales, don't check the box. If you're going to share e-commerce revenue, do check the box and outline the details of your agreement in Attachment F, discussed below. The advertising revenue sharing provisions should clearly state how and when payments to the licensor will be made. It's common for payments to be made either monthly or quarterly, with the payment due 30 days after the end of the month or quarter.*

8. Term and Termination

8.1 *Initial Term.* This Agreement takes effect on _____ (the Effective Date). Unless the Agreement is terminated sooner as provided below, it will remain effective for an Initial Term of _____ months.

8.2 *Renewal.* After the Initial Term, this Agreement will be automatically renewed for successive additional _____ -month periods (Extension Terms). Either party, however, may prevent a renewal from taking effect by notifying the other party at least 60 days before the end of the Initial Term or an Extension Term.

8.3 *Performance Prevented.* If a party cannot perform any of its obligations due to a cause beyond the reasonable control of the party, that party's performance will be excused and the time for performance will be extended for the period of delay or inability to perform due to such occurrence.

8.4 *Termination.* Either party may terminate this Agreement if the other party:

(a) fails to make timely payments as provided in this Agreement, and does not remedy the failure within 30 days after being notified in writing, or

(b) breaches any material obligations under this Agreement, and does not remedy the breach within 30 days after being notified in writing.

8.5 *Effect of Termination.* Unless terminated for cause, any termination under this Section 8 will be without any liability or obligation of the terminating party. The provisions of Sections 8, 9, 10 and 11 will survive termination of this Agreement.

Explanation: *Follow the instructions in the section on Affiliate Licenses above (Section B).*

9. Indemnification

Licensee will indemnify Licensor, its employees, directors, agents and affiliates, against any third-party claim or proceeding brought against Licensor that is based on or arises from any unauthorized deletions, additions or alterations to, or any unauthorized use of, any Licensed Content or Licensor Brand Features made by Licensee. Licensee will pay any and all costs, damages and expenses, including reasonable attorneys' fees and costs awarded against or otherwise incurred by Licensor in connection with or arising from any such claim, suit or proceeding.

Licensor will indemnify Licensee, its employees, directors, agents and affiliates, against any claim or proceeding brought against Licensee that is based on or arises from any third-party claim that the Licensed Content or any Licensor Brand Feature infringes any Intellectual Property Right or contains any material or information that is defamatory or violates any third party's right of publicity or privacy or has otherwise resulted in any tort, injury, damage or harm to any person. Licensor will pay any and all costs, damages and expenses, including reasonable attorneys' fees and costs awarded against Licensee in connection with or arising from any such claim or proceeding.

Licensee is not required to edit or review any Licensed Content for accuracy or appropriateness.

Explanation: *We explain indemnification above in The Affiliate Agreement (Section 10) in Section B. Here is an example of how indemnification may affect the parties to a Content License.*

Example: *Organicsolutions.com licenses its health and nutrition content to healthyoptions.com. The content license agreement includes a provision indemnifying HealthyOptions against any damages awarded against HealthyOptions based on its use of OrganicSolutions content. Dr. Smith, author of a popular diet book, visits healthyoptions.com, reads the content and finds defamatory statements about herself. She sues HealthyOptions for damages. The jury awards a large verdict against HealthyOptions, but since OrganicSolutions indemnified HealthyOptions, OrganicSolutions will have to pay the damages awarded to Dr. Smith—and the costs of the lawsuit as well.*

10. Limitation of Liability

NEITHER LICENSOR NOR LICENSEE WILL BE LIABLE TO THE OTHER PARTY FOR INDIRECT, INCIDENTAL, CONSEQUENTIAL, SPECIAL OR EXEMPLARY DAMAGES ARISING FROM THIS AGREEMENT, EVEN IF THAT PARTY HAS BEEN ADVISED OF THE POSSIBILITY OF SUCH DAMAGES, INCLUDING LOSS OF REVENUE OR ANTICIPATED PROFITS OR LOST BUSINESS.

Explanation: *This clause is explained in The Affiliate Agreement (Section 11) in Section B.*

11. Ownership

11.1 *By Licensor.* Licensee acknowledges and agrees that:

Licensor owns all right, title and interest in the Licensed Content and the Licensor Brand Features.

Nothing in this Agreement confers in Licensee any right of ownership in the Licensed Content or the Licensor Brand Features.

Licensee will not contest Licensor's ownership or the validity of the Licensor Brand Features.

Licensee will not assert any other association with Licensor other than as expressed in this Agreement.

All uses and accompanying good will of the Licensor Brand Features belong to Licensor.

11.2 *By Licensee.* Licensor acknowledges and agrees that:

Licensee owns all right, title and interest in the Licensee Property which consists of Licensee Brand Features and other Intellectual Property Rights of Licensee, including the look and feel of the Licensee website.

Nothing in this Agreement confers in Licensor any license or right of ownership in the Licensee Property.

Licensor will not contest the ownership or validity of the Licensee Property.

Explanation: *See Section B2 for an explanation of this clause.*

12. Public Announcements

The parties will cooperate to create appropriate public announcements relating to the relationship set forth in this Agreement. Neither party will make any public announcement regarding the existence or content of this Agreement without the other party's prior written approval.

Explanation: *This clause is explained in The Affiliate Agreement (Section 13) in Section B2.*

13. Disputes

(Choose One)

❑ Mediation. If a dispute arises, the parties will try in good faith to settle it through mediation conducted by:

❑ _____

❑ a mediator to be mutually selected.

The parties will share the costs of the mediator equally. Each party will cooperate fully and fairly with the mediator and will attempt to reach a mutually satisfactory resolution to the dispute. If the dispute is not resolved within 30 days after it is referred to the mediator, either party may take the matter to court.

❑ Mediation and Possible Arbitration. If a dispute arises, the parties will try in good faith to settle it through mediation conducted by:

_____

❑ a mediator to be mutually selected.

The parties will share the costs of the mediator equally. Each party will cooperate fully and fairly with the mediator and will attempt to reach a mutually satisfactory solution to the dispute. If the dispute is not resolved within 30 days after it is referred to the mediator, it will be arbitrated by:

❑ _____

❐ an arbitrator to be mutually selected.

Judgment on the arbitration award may be entered in any court that has jurisdiction over the matter. The arbitrator will allocate costs of arbitration, including attorney fees.

Explanation: *Provisions 13 through 22, which are standard in most contracts, are explained in Chapter 3, Section F.*

14. Relationships

This Agreement does not make either party a partner, joint venturer or employee of the other party.

15. Invalid Provisions

If a court finds any provision of this Agreement invalid or unenforceable, the remainder of this Agreement will be interpreted so as best to carry out the parties' intent.

16. Entire Agreement

This is the entire Agreement between the parties. It replaces and supersedes any oral agreements between the parties, as well as any prior writings.

17. Modification

Any modifications to this Agreement must be in writing.

18. Waiver

The failure to exercise any right in this Agreement will not waive prior or subsequent rights.

19. Notices

All notices must be in writing. A notice may be delivered to a party at the address the party designates in writing. A notice may be delivered:

a. in person

b. by certified mail, or

c. by overnight courier.

20. Successors and Assigns

This agreement binds and benefits the heirs, successors and assigns of the parties.

21. Attorney Fees and Expenses

If there is litigation, the prevailing party may collect from the other party its reasonable costs and attorney fees incurred in enforcing this Agreement.

22. Governing Law

This Agreement will be governed by and construed in accordance with the laws of the state of _____.

Dated: _____

LICENSOR:

Name of Business:

_____

A _____

By: _____

Printed Name and Title:_____

Address:_____

LICENSEE:

Name of Business:

_____

A _____

By: _____

Printed Name and Title:_____

Address:_____

Explanation: *For information on how to handle signatures, see Chapter 3, Section F4.*

Attachment A
Licensed Content

LICENSOR BRAND FEATURES

Licensor business name: _____

Related logos: _____

Any other business names used by Licensor: _____

Related logos: _____

LICENSEE BRAND FEATURES

Licensor business name: _____

Related logos: _____

Any other business names used by Licensor: _____

Related logos: _____

Explanation: *Use Attachment A to describe what content will be licensed. Make sure the content is described in enough detail to prevent confusion over what pieces or excerpts the Licensee wants to use. Also list the Licensee and Licensor's brand features (trademarks) that are related to the transaction. These generally include the business names of each party, their website addresses if different from the business name and any related logos.*

EXAMPLE:

Attachment A
Licensed Content

Article titled, "Celebrate *No Rooz,* Persian New Year," by Parisha Heydari, from the March, 2001 issue of *la cocinita* magazine.

LICENSOR BRAND FEATURES

la cocinita magazine

la cocinita magazine related logos

lacocinita.com

lacocinita.com related logos

LICENSEE BRAND FEATURES

WorldHolidays.com

WorldHolidays.com related logos

Attachment B

Fees

The fee of $_____ for the _____ initial term year will be paid on signing of this Agreement. Thirty days prior to any renewal, Licensor will pay Licensee a non-refundable licensing fee of $_____ for each renewal term.

Attachment C

Branding and Links

During the Term of this Agreement, Licensee will maintain the following links:

Location of Link	Specifics of Link	Link to Where
At the top of all Content Pages containing Licensed Content.	Licensor logo, with dimensions of no less than [dimensions]. pixels.	The home page of Licensor's own website.
At the beginning of the Licensed Content on each Content page.	Text link stating "From Licensed Content on the [Licensor] site," in the same type size as the body text of the Content.	The related area of the Licensor website.
In appropriate locations on the Content Pages as provided by Licensor.	Text links to related topics and information on the Licensor website.	Pages within the Licensor website that are directly related to the Licensed Content and pages within other sites with appropriate content.
At the end of the Licensed Content on each Content Page.	Text link stating "Click here for related information and products from [Licensor]," in the same type size as the body text of the Content.	The related area of the Licensor website.
At the bottom of all pages containing licensed content	Text link as part of copyright attribution stating "Copyright" [year] [licensor]	The home page of licensor's own website.

Explanation: *If the requirements for the branding and linking are lengthy or detailed (as is often the case), it's a good idea to include them in a separate attachment to the contract. Use Attachment C to specify in detail how the Licensee will present Licensor brand features, logos and links to the content owner's site. We've provided some common placement requirements in our standard agreement, but you may amend or delete any of them to fit your needs.*

Attachment D
Delivery and Technical Specifications

A. Licensor's Responsibilities

1. Licensor will have the sole responsibility for Licensed Content creation and maintenance.

2. Licensor will supply Licensee with updates to the content covered under this Agreement as they become available.

B. Licensee's Responsibilities

1. Licensee will present the information on pages consistent with Licensee's user interface.

2. Licensee will be responsible for providing continuous links as set out in paragraph 3.6 and Attachment C of this Agreement.

C. Format of Content Delivery:

Licensor will deliver Content to Licensee via FTP or email feed in HTML, XML, CSV or Tab-delimited text file format.

Explanation: *This attachment outlines the responsibilities of the parties for delivering, maintaining and updating the content. If the content won't need updating—for example, fine art photographs, drawings or poems—you may delete the language in A.2 regarding the content owner's responsibility to submit updates.*

[Optional] Attachment E
Advertising Revenue Sharing

1. Definition

Net Advertising Revenue means all revenue from advertising and sponsorships that appears on Content Pages.

2. Agreement to Share Advertising Revenue

2.1 *Commissions.* Licensee will pay Licensor _____% of the Net Advertising Revenue that accrues to Licensee during the term of this Agreement from advertising and sponsorships that appear on Content Pages.

2.2 *Payments.* Payments by Licensee to Licensor will be made _____monthly _____quarterly, due within _____days of the end of each _____ calendar month _____ quarter. With each payment, Licensee will provide to Licensor documentation reasonably detailing the calculation of the payment.

2.3 *Responsibility for Selling Advertising.* Licensee will be solely responsible for selling any advertising on the Licensee Site.

3. Audits and Reports

3.1 *Records and Inspections.* Licensee will maintain accurate records with respect to the calculation of all payments due under this Agreement. Licensor and its representative may, upon at least _____ days' prior written notice to Licensee, and no more than once per year, inspect Licensee records reasonably related to the calculation of such payments during Licensee's normal business hours. If an inspection reveals any underpayment of fees by Licensee of greater than _____%, Licensee will promptly reimburse Licensor for all costs of the audit along with the amount due with interest on such sums.

3.2 *Usage Reports.* Licensee will send to Licensor, via email, usage reports containing the total number of page views generated by Content Pages. Each usage report will cover a calendar [month] [quarter] and will be delivered within _____ days following the end of the applicable _____ calendar month _____quarter.

4. Competitor Advertising

4.1 Licensee will not sell, allow to be sold, post or allow to be posted on Content Pages any advertising of the following Competitors of Licensor:

4.2 Upon _____days' written notice to Licensee, Licensor may expand the list of Competitors to reflect any ventures that Licensor was unaware of when this Agreement was signed.

Explanation: *If you won't be sharing advertising revenues, then don't include this attachment; simply re-letter the following attachments accordingly.*

If you are going to share ad revenues, this attachment will contain the details of your arrangement. Enter the commission percentage—that is, the percentage of any revenue from advertising that appears on pages with licensed content—that the Licensee will pay the Licensor. A rate of 50% of net advertising revenue is common, though it will depend on the bargaining power of the parties (as always) and how valuable the content is.

Next, spell out the payment arrangements: whether payments will be made monthly or quarterly and how long after the end of each period they are due; ten, 15 or 20 days is common. Make similar arrangements for delivery of the usage reports.

Content owners typically want to make sure that the Licensee keeps good track of advertising revenues to ensure that the payments being made are fair and accurate. It's good practice to require the Licensee to keep adequate records, and to give the content owner the right to occasionally inspect those records after giving adequate notice. Another option is to provide that the Licensee will pay for an audit if the content owner discovers that it had been underpaid. [This issue is also discussed in the Explanation for Attachment F.]

In the Reports and Audits section, enter how much notice the Licensor must give before inspecting the Licensee's records; 30 days is typical. Then enter what percentage of underpayments will trigger penalty provisions; 5% or 10% is common.

A content owner obviously won't want a Licensee to permit any competitor to advertise on pages of licensed content. It's a good idea to include a provision that prohibits competitor advertising in the ad revenue sharing terms. A prohibition on competitor advertising can refer to a list of known competitors, which the content owner may update periodically as new competitors may enter the market. In the Competitor Advertising section, enter the number of days' notice that will be required for the Licensor to add to the list of competitors (which will be in Attachment F). A 30-day notice period is generally adequate and typical.

[Optional] Attachment F
E-Commerce Revenue Sharing

1. Definitions

• Qualified Purchases are those that (a) are purchased by users of the Licensor site who come from the Licensee site via a text link or a hyperlinked GIF, (b) that are sold and shipped by Licensor, and (c) for which Licensor has received full payment.

• Net Sales means the aggregate amount actually paid to Licensor for Qualified Purchases, excluding sales taxes, shipping, handling and other similar charges, amounts due to credit card fraud, and bad debt and credits for returned goods.

2. Agreement to Share E-Commerce Revenue

Licensee will receive a commission on Qualified Purchases of Licensor products generated by Licensee site users.

The Licensee agrees to display within the navigation section of all Licensed Content Pages a hyperlinked graphical image, (a "hyperlinked GIF") with dimensions of no less than _____ x _____ pixels, of a related Licensor product.

3. Commissions

The commission rate on all Licensor products will be _____% of Net Sales for Qualified Purchases. Commission rates will be based on Net Sales. Commissions will be paid to the Licensee in U.S. dollars_____monthly _____quarterly, _____days after the end of the _____month_____quarter, and mailed with a detailed Sales Report for that period.

The Licensee is eligible to earn commissions only on sales occurring during the term outlined in Sections 8.1 and 8.2 of this Agreement. Commissions earned through the date of termination will remain payable only if the related Licensor product orders are not canceled or returned. Licensor may withhold the Licensee's final payment for a reasonable time to ensure that the correct amount is paid.

4. Records, Sales Reports and Audits

Both parties will maintain accurate records with respect to the calculation of all payments due under this Agreement. Licensor will provide Licensee with monthly Sales Reports, by the _____day of each month.

Once per year, Licensee will have the right, upon no less than _____days' prior written notice, to appoint an independent third party to audit Licensor's books and records during regular business hours in order to verify compliance with the terms of this Agreement. Any such audit will be conducted in a manner that does not unreasonably interfere with Licensor's business activities. Such audit will be at Licensee's expense; however, if the audit reveals overdue payments in excess of _____% of the payments owed to date, Licensor will promptly pay the cost of such audit, and Licensee may conduct another audit during the same one-year period.

5. Customer Relations and Policies

Customers who buy products from Licensor via a hyperlinked GIF will be considered to be customers of Licensor. All Licensor rules, policies and operating procedures concerning customer orders, customer service, and Licensor product sales will apply to these customers. Licensor reserves the right to change its products, prices, policies and operating procedures at any time. Licensor will use all commercially reasonable efforts to provide the Licensee with accurate product information, but cannot guarantee the availability or price of any particular product.

Explanation: *If you'll be sharing e-commerce revenue, enter the specifics of your arrangement here. If you don't plan to share revenue from online sales, then don't include this attachment.*

The site selling products or services will almost always want to deduct certain costs from its total sales revenues before calculating the referring site's percentage. In other words, the referring site's commission won't be based on the sales site's total income, but on its revenue minus certain expenses, such as shipping, bad debts or sales taxes. The definition of net sales can be the subject of significant negotiation. The seller would like to deduct as much as possible before calculating the commission; the referring site will always want fewer deductions made before its gets its cut.

Enter the size, in pixels, of any required graphical images the Licensee must display to promote the content owner's products or services. Next, enter the commission percentage that the Licensee will earn on each sale, typically 5% or 10%. Then choose whether payments will be sent monthly or quarterly, and state how many days after the end of the month or quarter the payments will be due (usually 30, 60 or 90 days).

How to Limit Your Liability

A business of any kind carries some legal risk, and online businesses have a few extra. It's not possible to remove risk entirely, but it can be reined in and kept to a minimum. This whole book, of course, is designed to keep you out of legal trouble. This chapter focuses on some strategies to limit your personal liability for business debts and to reduce losses to the business itself. Some of these tried-and-true strategies aren't unique to companies doing business online. But because e-commerce poses some new and unsettled legal issues, the strategies in this chapter take on added importance. Here's what we recommend:

- **Strategy #1—Create a corporation or limited liability company (LLC).** If you organize your business as a corporation or LLC, you'll go a long way toward protecting your personal (non-business) assets if someone sues your business and gets a judgment against it. Generally speaking, your home, bank and car will be safe from business creditors and anyone hurt in the course of business operations.

- **Strategy #2—Set up a separate legal entity for your online business.** This strategy can save a healthy part of your business from being brought to its knees by an unhealthy part. For example, if you have a highly successful brick-and-mortar business, you can protect it from being ruined

by a hefty judgment against your website business.

- **Strategy #3—Carry adequate insurance.** Many online legal risks can be covered by insurance, but traditional business insurance policies may not do the trick. Fortunately, policies are now available to cover many of the risks peculiar to e-commerce.

- **Strategy #4—Avoid getting sued in another state or different country.** With an online business, you may suddenly find yourself doing business in other states, and maybe even in foreign countries. If you're sued, courts in those places may gain jurisdiction over your business, forcing you to defend yourself in unfamiliar places that operate under unfamiliar laws and rules. We'll show you how to reduce that risk.

- **Strategy #5—Use contracts to limit liability.** In a well-written contract—whether it's entered into using paper and ink or formed online—your customers, clients and others can agree that your liability to them is limited. For example, if you're selling computers online, the buyer can agree that if the product breaks down, your liability will be limited to replacing the computer or refunding the purchase price. If you use the right wording, you won't be responsible for other losses (such as the buyer's lost income) resulting from the computer's failure.

Any one of these strategies can save you or your business from financial ruin. By combining two or more of them, you can erect a strong legal shield against the perils of doing business online. Put all of them to work for you and you'll sleep very well indeed.

A. Creating a Corporation or LLC

Every business is a legal entity of some kind. The most popular forms for a small business are a sole proprietorship, partnership, corporation or limited liability company (LLC).

Many factors should influence your choice. But we recommend that you strongly consider using either a corporation or an LLC for your online business, for one simple reason: it will limit your personal liability for business obligations. If you're doing business as a sole proprietorship or partnership, many personal assets could be taken to satisfy a business debt. By contract, if a court judgment is entered against your corporation or LLC, you stand to lose only the money you've invested.

1. How Your Liability Is Limited

If you organize your business as either a corporation or LLC, your business will be legally separate from the people who own or operate it. That's true even if you have a one-person business, in which you're the only owner and the only employee. Because the business is a separate entity, you will not, with some exceptions, be personally liable for legal obligations incurred by it.

Generally, as long as you've acted only as an officer or director of your corporation or as a member or manager of your LLC, a creditor who wins a lawsuit against the business can't touch your personal bank accounts, your home and other valuable property you own. So if you sign for a corporate loan as president of the company rather than as an individual, you're not personally responsible for repaying the debt if the business runs out of money. Similarly, you don't have to pay if someone is injured because of business activities, as long as you didn't cause the injury.

EXAMPLE: Ed and Marnie form Industrial Solutions Inc., a chemical company that packages and ships solvents to customers, many of whom place orders on the company's website. One day, an Industrial Solutions employee mislabels one shipment of a volatile solvent, resulting in severe chemical burns to three workers at the purchaser's company. The workers sue and win a huge judgment against Industrial Solutions. Because Industrial Solutions is a corporation, only corporate assets are available to pay the damages. Ed and Marnie are not personally liable.

You can be liable, however, for your own negligence (carelessness that's unreasonable under the circumstances). If Ed himself rather than an employee had mislabeled the shipment, the fact that the business is a corporation wouldn't protect him from personal liability. He'd be liable for his negligence or for other wrongs (called torts, in legal lingo) that he personally committed. And no doubt any person injured by Ed's negligence would sue and be able to collect from both Ed and the corporation.

Banks and major companies are well aware that the personal assets of the corporation's owners are protected if the company has bills it can't pay or a loan payment it can't meet. As a result—especially if you have a new business or one without an exemplary credit history—a bank may not lend money to your business unless you and the other owners sign a guarantee promising to be liable for the debt. Similarly, a big company may not let your corporation or LLC buy goods on credit unless all of the corporate or LLC owners guarantee payment. And if you guarantee payment, your personal assets will be on the line if the company can't pay the debt.

So in the real world, the limited liability you enjoy by forming a corporation or LLC has its greatest value in protecting you from:

- Debts that you haven't personally guaranteed, such as most routine bills for supplies and small items of equipment, and payments owed to independent contractors hired by the corporation or LLC.
- Injuries (both physical and financial) caused by corporate or LLC activities that are not fully covered by insurance, and
- The consequences of misdeeds or bad judgment of your co-owners. By contrast, in a partnership, each partner is personally liable for the business-related activities of the other partners.

⚠ Make sure the payroll taxes get paid. Limited liability won't protect you from personal liability if your corporation or LLC fails to deposit taxes withheld from employees' wages—especially if you have anything to do with making decisions about what bills the company pays first. Also, because unpaid withheld taxes can't be discharged in bankruptcy, you want to pay these before you pay other debts (most of which can be wiped out in bankruptcy) in case your business goes downhill.

Corporations and LLCs: Terminology

	Corporation	LLC
Owners are called . . .	Shareholders	Members
Owner owns . . .	Shares of Stock	Membership Interest
You create it by filing . . .	Articles of Incorporation (or, in some states, Certificate of Incorporation or Charter)	Articles of Organization
You spell out internal operating procedures in . . .	Bylaws	Operating Agreement

2. Choosing Between an LLC or a Corporation

Which is better for your business, a corporation or an LLC? No one answer applies to every business. Nevertheless, for many e-commerce businesses, the relative simplicity, flexibility and lower cost of the LLC make it the better choice.

There are, however, other factors that may tip the balance toward a corporation. Consider a corporation if:

- **You want to entice or keep key employees by offering stock options and stock bonus incentives.** LLCs don't have stock; corporations do. While it's possible to reward an employee by offering a membership interest in an LLC, the process is awkward and likely to be less attractive to the employee.

- **You want to attract investors.** You could offer investors a membership interest in an LLC, but they'd much prefer to have stock. And it's relatively simple for a corporation to adjust to different investment scenarios by issuing classes of stock with different benefits and restrictions.

- **You'd like to provide extensive fringe benefits to owner-employees.** Often, when you form a corporation, you expect to be both a shareholder (owner) and an employee. The corporation can, for example, hire you to serve as its CEO and pay you a tax-deductible salary. But corporate owners don't just receive pay; most also receive fringe benefits. These benefits can include the payment of health insurance premiums and direct reimbursement of medical expenses. The corporation can deduct the cost of these benefits, and they're not treated as taxable income to the employees. Having your own corporation pay for these fringe benefits and deduct the cost as a business expense can be an attractive feature of doing business as a corporation. These opportunities for you to receive tax-favored benefits are somewhat reduced if you do business as an LLC. Also, a corporation may be able to offer slightly better retirement benefits or options under a corporate retirement plan. (Be aware that the tax rules are different for a special kind of corporation called the S Corporation. Your tax advisor can explain.)

For more information on selecting a business entity and the mechanics of creating a corporation or LLC, see *Legal Guide for Starting or Running a Small Business*, by Fred S. Steingold (Nolo).

B. Making Your Online Business a Separate Legal Entity

If you have a brick-and-mortar business and are planning to expand by selling goods or services online, one possibility is to use a single business entity for both arms of the business. For example, if your existing business is set up as a corporation, there's no reason why you can't use that same corporation to run your online operations. It's done all the time.

But if you do that, and your online operations happen to incur huge debts or get hit by a huge lawsuit, creditors could go after any of the corporation's assets to pay the debt or lawsuit judgment, including the company's general bank accounts and other property. There's a way around this, although it requires more paperwork and some special care in how you conduct your business: You can set up a separate legal entity just for your online business. If you do that and follow a few basic precautions, the liabilities of the online business won't bring down your established business.

EXAMPLE: Office Stuff Inc. has been in business for 25 years and has a loyal regional following. Thinking that its selection of high-tech, high-end office supplies could have a national market, Office Stuff decides to go online. It creates Office Surprise LLC as a separate business.

Unfortunately, the new e-commerce business has difficulty surviving online. A large order is botched and the unhappy customer sues and obtains a $300,000 judgment against the LLC, none of which is covered by insurance. Office Surprise LLC can't pay the judgment and has to shut down. But since it's a separate legal entity, the original business (Office Stuff Inc.) isn't affected and continues to thrive.

This strategy works both ways, of course. Your physical store may find itself on the ropes while your online business is prospering. Again, if you have separate entities, you can walk away from the brick-and-mortar operation without putting your online business in jeopardy.

Another benefit of using a separate legal entity for your online business is that you may have a different set of owners involved. For example, you and Spencer may own the brick-and-mortar operation while you, Rich and Mary may want to own the e-commerce venture. That's easily accomplished by using the two-entity strategy described here.

Now, about the precautions. To keep one business free from the legal liabilities of the other, you must scrupulously run the businesses as separate entities. If you blur the line between the two, a judge may view the strategy as a sham and treat both companies as one, meaning the assets of both can be taken to satisfy the debts of either. Obviously, that would defeat the whole purpose of having separate companies.

At the very least, you need to maintain separate bank accounts and separate payrolls for the two businesses. In signing contracts, make sure the right business is named and that you sign on behalf of the business—for example: Office Stuff Inc., a California corporation by John Gray, President *or* Office Surprise LLC, a California limited liability company by John Gray, Member. Maintain separate stationery, business forms and signs for the two companies. Establish separate phone and fax numbers. Finally, if the two companies will be doing business with each other, prepare and sign contracts between defining the terms of the relationship. Your goal is to emulate what you'd do if the companies had no overlapping ownership.

Obviously, running two companies adds expense, which makes this strategy too costly for the smallest of businesses. And the separate paperwork can become a headache when the same employees work for both entities, or products are sold from the same stock of goods. In the above example, the e-commerce business might agree to buy supplies from Office Stuff Inc. to fill its orders, in which case keeping track of how one entity pays the other could become a hassle.

C. Carrying Adequate Insurance

Most businesses—even very small ones—buy insurance to protect them from business catastrophes. But traditional business insurance policies may not adequately protect your e-commerce operations. You need to look into more specialized coverage, which, fortunately, is now widely available.

Two kinds of insurance are essential:

- **Property insurance** covers damage to the space where you do business and to your computers, furnishings, inventory and supplies. For example, if a fire destroys your office, the insurance will cover the cost of restoring the office and replacing your computers and other tangible assets. Of course, you'll probably have to pay a deductible, and every policy places a cap on the total amount the insurance company will pay.
- **Liability insurance** covers claims and lawsuits by people or businesses that have suffered physical or financial losses because of your business activities. This would include, for example, a claim by a computer repair specialist who trips on a cable in your office, falls and breaks an ankle. As with property insurance, there may be a deductible for you to pay, and there'll be a cap on your coverage.

Many businesses find a third kind of insurance also helpful:

- **Business interruption insurance** covers losses you incur if you must temporarily curtail or cease operation because of a fire or flood. If your busi-

ness property is damaged or destroyed, and you have to shut down for two months while your premises are rebuilt and your equipment is replaced, you may lose substantial income and have to pay significant expenses in the interim. These losses and expenses are covered by business interruption insurance.

If you've been running a business, you probably have at least the first two types of insurance and maybe the third as well. But will your current insurance be sufficient for your e-commerce business? Maybe not. For example, your software may be damaged or destroyed, or you may lose data because of a virus, a hacker, a power surge or a careless or malicious employee. Your property insurance policy may not cover such electronic losses. And the partial shutdown of your business because of electronic mishaps may not be enough for your business interruption insurance to kick in.

Similarly, traditional liability coverage may not be extensive enough to cover e-commerce risks. For example, your liability policy may cover you if another business sues you for property damage, which is defined in the policy as "physical injury to or destruction of tangible property or loss of use of tangible property." But what if your business does something that makes a customer's computer crash, or you harm the customer's software or data? Will your business be covered? Again, maybe not, since the damage or loss may not be to *tangible* property.

And while your liability coverage may include business torts like defamation or copyright infringement, the policy language may be too narrow to include claims based on your e-commerce activities. Traditional policies lump these torts into a category intended for *advertising* activities. Having a website may or may not be treated as advertising under your liability policy.

So your job is to seek out cyber-insurance, coverage that recognizes the reality that electronic data is property and electronic losses are real losses. You also need insurance that covers you for such online torts as defamation, copyright and trademark infringement and invasion of privacy. Luckily, a growing number of insurance companies are now offering insurance policies that specifically cover e-commerce activities. For information about some of the coverage that's available, look at http://www.irmi.com/expert/articles/rossi004Chart.asp.

Each business has different insurance needs; it's important to analyze the specific risks for which your business needs coverage. One business may be mainly concerned about liability for the products it sells online. Another may worry about liability for possible invasions of privacy. Still another may want coverage in case it accidentally infringes on someone's copy-right or patent. Once you've figured out what you need, talk to an experienced insurance agent or broker. If your policy doesn't cover the e-commerce activities that your business engages in, it will be a waste of money.

Pay attention to the amount of the portion of each claim that you're obligated to pay (the *deductible*). By having a higher deductible, you can reduce the insurance premium.

D. Avoiding Out-of-State Lawsuits

One of the great things about having a website is that people everywhere can view it and do business with you online. One of the worst things about having a website is that people everywhere can, potentially, sue you in the courts of their home states or countries. Do you have to submit to far-flung courts' authority? So far, judges' answers to this question are far from consistent. In this section, we'll explain the problem and suggest ways to minimize your chances of being sued outside your own state.

1. The Basics of Jurisdiction

Jurisdiction is all about the power of a court to enter a legally binding judgment against you or your business. If your business is established in a certain state—for example, your headquarters are in Virginia—the courts of that state automatically have jurisdiction over your business. This means that someone can sue you there, and you're bound by the result.

But your home state may not be the only place you can be sued. Depending on the circumstances, courts in other states may have jurisdiction as well. In general terms, however, a court in another state won't have jurisdiction over your business unless you've had some contact or connection with that state. For example if you regularly travel to Colorado to sign contracts and conduct business there, and your contacts with Colorado are significant (the legal term is *continuous and systematic*) the Colorado courts would probably have jurisdiction.

An out-of-state court may also have jurisdiction if the lawsuit arises out of or is related to contacts with the state where you're being sued. The person suing you must show that you "purposefully directed" your activities at residents of the state where you're being sued—for example, that you deliberately and falsely disparaged a business in another state.

States typically have a *long-arm statute* that lists certain kinds of contacts with the state that are sufficient to give the state jurisdiction. If you haven't had the kinds of contacts listed in the statute, you'll

have a good chance of having a lawsuit dismissed for lack of jurisdiction.

2. Jurisdiction in E-Commerce Cases

Because state jurisdiction statutes have been around for many decades, courts have had ample opportunity to apply them, and it's relatively easy to gauge when an out-of-state court will have jurisdiction over a traditional business. The going gets tougher when a company is transacting business in cyberspace. But several courts have adopted a legal test first set out in 1997.

In this case, Zippo Manufacturing, best known for its cigarette lighters, brought a trademark infringement lawsuit in federal court in Pennsylvania against a California corporation that had been using the name Zippo for its Internet news service. Customers who wanted access to the Zippo news service applied online and paid by credit card either online or by phone. Then they got a password that let them download messages that were stored on a server in California. All of the California company's contacts with Pennsylvania were through the Internet. Of some 140,000 paying customers, 3,000 were Pennsylvania residents. Using a novel test, the court concluded it had jurisdiction. (*Zippo Manufacturing Co. v. Zippo Dot Com Inc.*, 952 F. Supp. 1119 (W.D. Pa. 1997).)

The *Zippo* test examines the nature and quality of commercial activity over the Internet. The test uses three general categories:

- **Passive Sites.** A passive site is one that simply posts information and doesn't take orders online. Basically, you're advertising on the Internet. This is treated like placing an ad in a national magazine. Generally, if nothing more is involved, the mere fact that a resident of another state can get access to your site isn't enough to let the courts of that state exercise jurisdiction over you.

- **Repeated Transmissions.** At the other end of the scale is a business that clearly does business over the Internet. If, for example, your business repeatedly transmits computer files over the Internet to residents of another state and enters into contracts with them, the other state almost certainly will have jurisdiction over your business.

- **The Interactive Middle Ground.** Between the two extremes lies a broad middle ground. Here, the website is interactive and permits the exchange of information between the company and website users. If your website falls into this category, your business may or may not be subject to the jurisdiction of an out-of-state court. It will depend on the level of interactivity and the commercial nature of the information exchanged. A limited exchange of emails, for example, or having forms that a user can download, may not constitute a sufficient basis for jurisdiction. But if you're doing business online with residents of the other state—selling them products, for example—you probably will be subject to jurisdiction there.

In giving their reasons for finding jurisdiction or the lack of it, judges try to hew to formulas like the *Zippo* one or the one that asks whether or not you've "purposefully directed" your website at residents of the state in which you're being sued. But all these tests leave considerable room for judicial discretion. Often, the judge can go either way. In those cases, if the nature of the website is offensive to the judge or the business's conduct is disturbing, the judge may find jurisdiction. Businesses with websites that feature sexual content, involve gambling or disparage religion may have difficulty in avoiding jurisdiction in another state's courts. Ditto for businesses with websites directed at children—or those being sued for an alleged consumer scam, defamation or the sale of a product that causes injury. Whether or not you think that's fair, you need to accept it as a reality and plan accordingly.

⚠ Take any summons seriously. If your business is served with a summons saying you've been sued in an out-of-state court, don't ignore it. You must take some action, even if you think it's preposterous to be sued there. If you do nothing, the court may issue a default judgment against you, and you may not be able to get that judgment dropped once it's been issued. Your business assets, and maybe your personal assets as well, will be at risk when the person or business that sued you goes to collect on the judgment.

Carefully check the summons to see the deadline for responding. If there's enough time, call the person who's suing you or the lawyer who prepared the papers. See if you can negotiate a settlement or perhaps get an agreement to have the dispute mediated or arbitrated. Otherwise, you'll have to hire a lawyer in the state where you've been sued to ask the court to dismiss the case for lack of jurisdiction. If the court refuses, and the stakes are high, your lawyer can file an appeal. But if you don't get the case knocked out on jurisdictional grounds, you'll have to hunker down and fight the case there on the merits.

3. Steps to Avoid Faraway Jurisdiction

There are steps you can take to reduce the chances of having to defend your business in a courtroom far from your home base, though there's no guarantee that these techniques will protect you completely. The downside of using these strategies is that to reduce your risk of being sued, you may limit your potential market for some customers. If you feel the odds are high that your business will get sued—perhaps you sell a product that's potentially hazardous—or if your aversion to risk is great, these techniques may be especially attractive. It's fine to go ahead and take the conservative route. But remember that in doing so, you're not making full use of the money-making possibilities that e-commerce offers.

💼 Since every business is different, it makes sense to discuss your jurisdiction protection plan with a lawyer. Sometimes, a slight shift in how you run your business can make a big difference in how your company will fare if you're sued away from home. A lawyer experienced in e-commerce or business litigation may be able to suggest operational changes that will give you more protection—and may have specific suggestions for what to say on your website. The cost of a consultation is well worth it if you're seeking to limit your litigation risks.

a. Opt for a Passive Site

The more passive your site, the less likelihood of distant lawsuits, as discussed in Section D2 above. You won't get the full benefit of an e-commerce site—but you will achieve greater peace of mind.

b. Don't Post Defamatory Material

You should never post something defamatory (something that damages someone's reputation), because you're likely to get sued for it. And a defamed person who lives in another state may be allowed to sue your business in that person's own state. The reason is that the effect of the defamation—injury to the person's reputation—is felt most intensely in the state where the defamed person lives.

c. Limit Your E-Commerce Activities to Residents of the U.S. or Other Selected Countries

If being sued in another state seems troubling to you, being sued in another country can be a downright nightmare. The laws and proceedings there may be much different than ours, and you may have the expense of traveling a great distance to defend your company. For most small businesses this issue will probably not

arise. If it does, the risk may be small, particularly if you don't have any assets or other business connection with the country. If you are concerned about being sued abroad, you should post a notice informing visitors to your website that your goods, services and information are offered only to United States residents —or residents of the U.S. and certain selected countries, such as Canada, perhaps. Then carefully monitor all orders to make sure they're all coming from the places you've listed, and reject those that aren't. If an entire transaction is handled online (with no mailing address) you may not know where the customer lives. But you can have customers acknowledge they live in the countries you've named— a step that should give you some protection. Also, look into filtering software; it may be effective in screening the origin of Internet communications.

If you do decide to deal with foreign residents, it's best to consult first with a lawyer well versed in international e-commerce law who can brief you on any special legal problems you need to be aware of.

d. Limit Your E-Commerce Activities to Your Own State

If you limit your e-commerce activities to residents of your own state or perhaps nearby states as well, you'll avoid having to fight a lawsuit in a distant state. Naturally, this limits your market, but maybe you can live with that if you're an extremely cautious person. The techniques you'd use are the same as suggested in subsection c above. Post a conspicuous notice. Then monitor your Internet activities carefully to be as certain as you can be that you are truly limiting the geographical scope of your business. Maybe you can't catch every customer who lives outside your target areas—but your efforts in trying to exclude more distant customers may be enough to avoid jurisdiction where you don't want to be.

e. Have Customers Agree That Only Your State Has Jurisdiction

Courts usually honor written contracts in which the parties have agreed on which state will have jurisdiction if there's a dispute. Courts are likely to honor such provisions in online contracts too. So you might insert such an understanding in a *click-through agreement*—the terms that a customer agrees to by clicking "I accept" or "I agree" when placing an order with you. Your click-through agreement might say that any dispute will be decided in the courts of your state and that the law of your state will apply.

But be aware that courts do not always honor jurisdiction provisions posted online. Chapter 6, Section F, explains the existing rules and contains an example of a jurisdiction provision.

f. Require Arbitration of Disputes

You may be able to avoid lawsuits altogether by having customers accept a click-through agreement requiring that disputes be decided by arbitration. And your click-thro··"⁄6₂ôreementquan specify that arbitration will take place in the county where your business is located and that the court there will have sole authority to enforce an arbitration award.

The combination of arbitration and local jurisdiction may get a bit more scrutiny from an out-of-state judge if the customer—especially a consumer—ignores the contract provision and sues you elsewhere. But you have a decent chance that it will be recognized and honored. It should be conspicuously presented in the agreement, not buried in small type.

E. Using Click-Through Agreements to Limit Liability

As explained in Chapters 11 and 12, the terms and conditions you post on your website can become contracts—especially if you require visitors and customers to click "I Agree" or "I Accept" before they can reach parts of your site, or purchase something. You can use your postings to limit the financial damages for which your business will be legally responsible if there's a problem with the products, services or information you offer online. It's true that language limiting your liability won't always have the desired effect; judges may balk at limitations that are grossly unfair or that try to cut off the amount a person can receive for bodily injuries. But in most situations, judges do enforce limitations that customers have agreed to.

Here's what one of your terms and conditions might look like:

PROTOBIZ WILL NOT BE LIABLE TO CUSTOMER FOR ANY DAMAGES BEYOND THE AMOUNT OF MONEY THAT CUSTOMER HAS ACTUALLY PAID TO PROTOBIZ.

When you use a limitation-of-liability clause in your posted terms and conditions, it's best to capitalize the entire clause. Some states require capital lettering in provisions such as this to give clear notice that one or both parties are giving up a legal right they're otherwise entitled to.

Attracting Customers

With all the companies battling for the same consumer dollars, how do you attract customers to your online business and effectively sell to them? Should you buy banner ads, print or radio ads, or try a promotional gimmick such as an online contest? It's one of the toughest challenges facing your e-business.

In this chapter, we'll review some of the methods that websites use to draw visitors to their sites. Then we'll advise you on how to stay out of legal trouble when you're wooing customers.

A. Strategies for Bringing People to Your Website

Before people can buy whatever you're selling online, they have to know your site exists, and come visit it. Several books (see below) and websites—for example, SelfPromotion.com (http://www.selfpromotion.com) and Traffik.com (http://www.traffik.com) are devoted to the subject of driving visitors to your site.

Many website promotion experts believe that the most important strategy for increasing traffic is to improve your ranking among search engines. Generally, the higher your company appears in the results of an Internet search, the more people you will attract. To increase your rankings you can invest in search engine software, buy "keywords" from a search engine so that your site appears higher in rankings when those words are entered by a searcher (see below) and make smart use of page titles and hidden codes known as meta tags at your site that are read by search engines. A website developer can help you design your site to be "search engine friendly."

The methodology of driving web traffic is constantly changing, and providing comprehensive advice on attracting and retaining customers is beyond the scope of this book. Here are some brief descriptions of some popular methods that you may wish to consider.

Buy keywords. GoTo and FindWhat (http://www.goto.com and http://www.findwhat.com) are among several search engines established on the principle that advertisers bid on placement in search results. In other words, a user of the GoTo search engine will be more likely to find your business if you have paid GoTo to be associated with a specific keyword—for example, "flowers" if you are a florist. This can be very cheap or very expensive—but done intelligently, it can attract high-quality traffic to your site for not much money. You can also purchase keywords from RealNames.com (http://www.realnames.com). The RealNames keyword system differs from the GoTo system in that a user can simply type a single word or phrase into the Internet Explorer browser—not a search engine—and access the related website.

(If you want to see how this works, type "powerpoint" or "chevron" into your Browser.)

Get links on other sites. You can pay for or swap links with other sites that draw the kinds of visitors you're looking for. We describe the mechanics of doing this in Chapter 7, Working With Other Websites.

Use your brick-and-mortar business to promote your website. You can put your domain name on your products, letterhead, store signs and packaging, and mention it in your voice-mail message. You can also include it in your Yellow Pages listing, and on company cars and trucks. You may even consider changing your business name to mirror your website—for example, as in the case of eKnitting.com, described in Chapter 1.

Encourage visitors to forward your site content to others. Look into "email this to a friend" software that makes it easy for visitors to pass along information originating on your site.

List your online business in directory sites, often called Yellow Pages directories. Like their paper-and-ink counterparts, these online directories are organized by subject, making it easy for someone who's looking for flowers or lamps or a resume-writing service to find you. One well-known site is http://www.555-1212.com. There are many others.

Send email to selected mailing lists. But be aware that unsolicited email, called spam, has a bad rep, and likely will be subjected to legal restrictions someday. See Section C, below.

Sponsor a contest or sweepstakes. Giveaways have to be carefully constructed, though, and you have to hew to numerous legal rules (see Section E, below). And while offering a prize may draw people to your site, there may be few among them who will become the customers you're looking for.

For more on how to attract customers, see *Increase Your Traffic in a Weekend,* by William Stanek (Prima Tech), and *Maximize Web Site Traffic,* by Robin Nobles and Susan O'Neil (Adams Media).

B. Avoiding Legal Problems When You Advertise

Legally speaking, the information you post on your site about your business and the products and services you offer is considered to be advertising. And so is the information you post on other websites or place in traditional print, radio and or TV media.

The basic legal rule for all advertising, whether it's online or off, is: Don't mislead or deceive consumers. Your advertisement will violate both federal and state laws if it tends to misinform or hoodwink the public. Taken as a whole, your ad must fairly inform the ordinary consumer. Any false statement of material fact that affects a consumer's decision to visit your site or purchase goods or services will violate the law, even if you didn't know the information was false.

The Federal Trade Commission (FTC) is the main federal agency that takes action against unlawful advertising. If FTC investigators believe that your online advertising violates the law, they'll probably try to bring you into voluntary compliance through informal means. They'll urge you, for example, to stop the offending practice, and to notify consumers who may have been misled. If that doesn't work, the agency can take legal action against your business, leading to court-enforced orders. To conserve its resources, the FTC usually focuses on larger companies and serious fraud, hoping the publicity about these cases will send a message to smaller companies. State and local governments can also go after your business and seek court orders prohibiting unlawful ads.

If you use misleading ads, you're more likely to be sued by a competitor than by the federal or state government. Companies often use a federal law called the Lanham Act to pursue competitors. If a competitor proves in court that your advertising is misleading, you may have to pay for its lost profits and lawsuit expenses. If a judge determines that you acted in bad faith and your behavior was particularly egregious—for example, you intentionally misled consumers in order to harm a competitor—the judge may increase the damage award to an amount up to three times the amount the competitor actually lost.

Keep in mind that advertising, for purposes of the Lanham Act, means more than traditional online ads; it's anything you say to influence consumers. It includes, for example:

- False statements on your website—for example an advertisement that falsely indicates your product outperforms a competitor's product.
- Hidden computer codes (known as meta tags) that misleadingly direct consumers to the website—for example, you use a competitor's name in your metatags and a consumer

seeking the competitor is mistakenly led to your site by a search engine.

- Email sent to consumers warning—falsely—that a competing product is deficient.
- False statements made by customer service representatives at your website that a competing company's product is unsafe.

The following rules will help keep your online ads within safe, legal limits. You won't get sued—and your customers will trust your business and recommend it to their friends.

1. Be Accurate

Because it's so important, we'll say it again: Make sure your ads are factually correct and don't tend to deceive or mislead the buying public. Don't show a picture of this year's model of a product if you're selling last year's model, even if they look almost the same. Be truthful about what consumers can expect from your product. Don't say that the software you're selling will work well with all personal computers when in fact it works well with only certain kinds.

Be sure that if challenged, you can substantiate the claims you make about your products. This is especially important when your claims concern health, safety or performance. And don't rely just on the claims a manufacturer makes. If you're selling the product online, you're responsible for the claims you make even if they came from the manufacturer. If the manufacturer's health or performance claims seem questionable, ask for documentation.

2. Get Permission

Does your ad feature someone's picture or endorsement? Does it quote material written by someone not employed by you or your advertising agency? Does it use the name of an organization such as the Sierra Club or Red Cross? If so, get written permission to use their picture or words. For information on obtaining permission, see Chapter 5.

Under U.S. copyright law, you can use limited quotations from copyrighted works without specific authorization from the copyright owner (see Chapter 5). In some circumstances, this provides legal justification for the widespread practice of quoting from favorable reviews in advertisements. However, with the exception of brief quotes from product or service reviews, you should always seek permission to quote protected material.

In addition, don't use any certification marks—for example the Good Housekeeping Seal of Approval—unless you have authority to do so and have checked the rules of use supplied by the organization that provides the certification.

3. Treat Competitors Fairly

A large percentage of false advertising lawsuits are based on comparative advertising, so don't knock the goods, services or reputation of others by giving false or misleading information. If you compare your goods and services with those of other companies, double-check your information to make sure that every statement in your ad is accurate. Then check again.

4. Have Sufficient Quantities on Hand

When you advertise goods for sale, make every effort to have enough on hand to supply the demand that it's reasonable to expect. If you don't think you can meet the demand, state in your ad that quantities are limited. You may even want to tell the number of units on hand.

5. Watch Out for the Word "Free"

If you say that goods or services are "free" or "without charge," be sure there are no unstated terms or conditions that qualify the offer. If there are any limits, state them clearly and conspicuously.

EXAMPLE: Bob owns an online hardware store and offers a free paintbrush to anyone who orders a can of paint for $8.95. If the $8.95 price is more than Bob usually charges for this kind of paint, the brush clearly

isn't free, and Bob has run afoul of FTC rules. Bob will also break the rules if he reduces the quality of the paint that the customer must purchase or the quantity of any services (such as free delivery) that he normally provides. By providing a lesser product or service, he's exacting a hidden cost for the brush.

In 2000, the FTC prohibited Office Depot, Buy.com and Value America from making offers for "free" and "low-cost" computers unless the ads informed consumers the true costs, particularly the requirement that the consumer sign up for three years of Internet access to get the "free" machine.

Do You Really Need to Advertise?

Besides what you post on your own website (legally, a form of advertising), you need to think about whether or not it pays to advertise elsewhere—especially when there are other marketing techniques available to build your online business (see Section A). It may be better to spend your money and efforts on providing top-notch service to each and every customer, so they'll give you repeat business and send more customers your way. To learn more on this subject, read *Marketing Without Advertising,* by Michael Phillips and Salli Rasberry (Nolo).

C. Spam

Sending unsolicited email to online customers who haven't elected to receive it is called *spamming*. From a marketing point of view, spam makes a lot of sense. Unlike junk mail, which is relatively expensive, there's little cost involved in spamming. Most legitimate businesses, however, avoid using spam because consumers hate it. Spam makes it harder and less pleasant for consumers to use the Web. It can overwhelm an unchecked mailbox in just a few days.

The marketplace perception is that most spam is aimed at perpetrating some sort of scam such as a pyramid scheme, a bogus stock offering, pirated software or quack health remedy. And much of it does involve deceptive practices. For example, spam for X-rated sites may be disguised with a personal subject header ("How come you didn't write back?" or "Here's my new email address") or even as anti-spam ("We Can Help Remove You From Spam Lists!"). In short, spam has become one of the most reviled forms of Internet communication. Stay away from it.

The law concerning spam is still in its infancy. But be aware that if you send spam, you may run into some serious hurdles. For one thing, an Internet Service Provider such as America Online (AOL) may block you from sending spam to its members. If you go to court to challenge the blocking on First Amendment grounds, you probably won't get very far. Courts haven't recognized a protected right to spam.

Anti-spam legislation has also been proposed in Congress and by 17 states, but so far only California and Washington have enacted tough anti-spam laws. California's law allows ISPs to sue spammers that violate an ISP's anti-spam policy and requires that commercial spam include opt-out instructions and, in some cases, an "ADV" (short for advertisement) at the beginning of the subject line (Cal. Bus. & Prof. Code §§ 17511.1 & 17538.45, Cal. Penal Code § 502). Washington's anti-spam law prohibits sending mail that uses a third party's Internet domain name without permission, or email that has a false or invalid return address, or contains a false or misleading header (Wash. Rev. Code § 19.190). It also permits an ISP to block messages which it believes are in violation of the law. The Washington Supreme Court has upheld the law and in 1998, a Washington man became the first person to recover damages under the law when he accepted a $200 payment as settlement for an unsolicited commercial email.

If you're sending out unsolicited commercial email, you can reduce your risk of violating an anti-spam law by following these precautions:

- Provide your name, email address and a toll-free phone number.

- Provide a simple way for the recipient to opt out of getting future email ads from you.
- Clearly indicate in the subject line that the email is an ad.

The air may be cleared if Congress passes one of the proposed laws now under consideration. For example, the Unsolicited Electronic Mail Act would require spammers to include a reply address, label the email as an ad and stop further emailing when requested. If passed, the Act would replace state anti-spam laws and set a national standard for unsolicited advertisements.

For current information on the state of spam laws, consult the website of the Coalition Against Unsolicited Commercial Email (http://www.cauce.org)

D. Alternatives to Spam: Permission Marketing

Not all bulk email is spam. Some is permission-based, meaning that the recipient has asked to receive it. This occurs when a user at a website agrees—for example, when making a purchase—to receive email or a newsletter (known as *opt-in email*). Unlike spam, opt-in email usually provides a benefit such as free informa-

tion or special offers. Here are some opt-in alternatives to spam:

- Invite people to subscribe to an email newsletter. Have a sign-up form on your website and explain that you'll send only timely, informative email to subscribers.
- Include late-breaking, useful information in the email you send to subscribers. Because it can be delivered so quickly, email is a perfect vehicle for alerting people who are already part of your community to new and interesting developments. Even a modestly self-serving message will go over well if you package it with some truly unique and valuable content. Just keep the hype to a minimum.
- Make it easy to quit receiving email. Every message should include brief, friendly instructions for getting off your mailing list. Even people who keep subscribing will appreciate knowing that you've made it easy for them to say, "Enough already!" when the time comes.

E. Contests and Sweepstakes

One powerful way to draw visitors to your website is to run a contest or sweepstakes. The possibility of winning a sizable prize is a strong incentive for many people. But unless you're selling ads on your site, traffic for traffic's sake may not help you. The people you attract through a contest or sweepstakes may not be interested in the goods and services you sell. And state laws strictly regulate these kinds of promotional events so be very careful before you start down this road.

We recommend that you visit a lawyer experienced in the laws of sweepstakes and contents if you are considering this kind of promotion. The devil is in the details, and there are too many to explain here.

1. Beware of Lotteries

It's against federal and state laws for businesses to run private lotteries. You must make sure that any promotion you run does not fit the definition of a lottery, which consists of these three basic elements:

- a prize
- awarded by chance
- to someone who pays something of value for a chance at winning.

If you sponsor a promotion that includes all three elements, you can expect to have it shut down by the authorities. You may have to pay a fine as well.

The way around this is to eliminate at least one of the three elements. Since you'll always be offering a prize, you must drop one of the other elements. Some possibilities:

- Award a prize based on the entrant's skill, not chance.
- Hold a sweepstakes, which people can enter for free.

Still, you may have to comply with complex laws covering contests and sweepstakes, which vary from state to state. Again, see a lawyer first.

2. Contests

If you sponsor a contest in which you award prizes based on skill and there is no luck involved, it's generally OK to require entrants to pay money or buy something from you. A few states, however, do require you to provide an alternate free method of entering.

Some state laws allow your contest to mix skill and luck, as long as the skill part weighs more heavily. Other states require that no luck be involved. So if you're going to accept entries nationwide, you need to make sure that chance plays no role in the contest.

EXAMPLE: Floriquest.com sponsors a contest in which entrants have to buy a Floriquest product and then correctly identify 20 flowers and plants pictured on the entry form. The winners will be drawn at random from the people who correctly name the pictured items. Since luck is involved in the final selection, this contest violates the laws of the states that ban any element of luck.

To be on the safe side, try to get rid of any element of luck in the process. Let's say your contest requires contestants to write an essay or come up with an advertising slogan. You should pick judges who will be qualified to judge the merit of the entries— and you should let entrants know what the criteria will be.

EXAMPLE: Floriquest.com sponsors a contest in which customers create a name for the company's new variety of rose bush and explain the reason for the name in 25 words or less. A horticulture professor, the head of a prominent ad agency and the author of a successful book on new media marketing will judge the entries. In judging, equal weight will be given to originality, sales appeal and appropriateness for use in both new and old media. These standards of comparison help assure that prizes will be awarded based on skill and not luck and the contest complies with state laws.

3. Sweepstakes

A sweepstakes is a game of chance: the luck of the draw. To avoid being considered an illegal lottery (see Section E1,

above), there can be no entrance fee or a requirement to purchase anything. Entrants must have an equal shot at winning a prize whether or not they buy something from you. It's smart to state conspicuously in the contest rules that no purchase is required.

An entry into a sweepstakes can involve a trivial cost. The cost of a postcard or a postage stamp, for example, has generally been regarded by regulators as too minor to be considered a cost of entry.

But what constitutes a free entry on the Internet is unclear. Some informed observers believe that the cost of computer equipment and Internet connection necessary to surf the Web is a real cost. Others disagree, pointing out that almost anyone can go to the library and use a computer for free.

It's hard to know how various states will ultimately resolve this issue. Also, regulators could find that even a nonmonetary requirement is actually a cost. For example, if someone must exert a substantial effort to enter the sweepstakes, it could be considered the same as paying to enter. This might happen if you required people to answer a long survey before they're eligible to enter or you require them to study information about your products. Even requiring them to submit to a long sales presentation could trigger a finding that entry really isn't free. So, obviously, you want to keep the entry requirements as simple and brief as possible.

For now at least, the practical answer is to offer a free, offline method for people to enter the sweepstakes. This is especially important if you're going promote your sweepstakes offline as well as online.

The alternate method—whether it's a postcard, fax or toll-free phone call—should have "equal dignity" with online entry. What that quaint legal phrase means is that you can't give online entrants any advantage. You need the same deadlines, for example, and the same pool of prizes. Also, be sure to clearly and conspicuously disclose the availability of the alternate free method.

 To stay current on laws on sweep stakes and contests, check the website sponsored by the law firm of Arent Fox at http://www.arentfox.com. (Select "Contests and Sweepstakes" from their "Special Focus" section.)

4. Disclosures

To give yourself the best chance of avoiding legal problems, you should disclose the rules of contests and sweepstakes as fully and clearly as possible. Here are some of the disclosures you should make:

- *How to enter.* Let entrants know all the ways they can submit an entry—for example, email, fax or postcard.
- *Starting and ending dates for entries.* Since you may get entries from various time zones, be specific about the time. To avoid disputes, say, for example, "All entries must be received by 8 p.m., Eastern Standard Time, December 1, 20XX."
- *Any limits on entries.* Maybe a person can only enter once or there can be only one entry per household. If so, say so. Also, spell out any limits on the age of entrants (you may want to disqualify people under 18 to avoid conflicts with some state laws) and on geographic area (you may want to avoid entries from outside the U.S. where different laws apply, and also

from states with especially stringent requirements.).

- *Details about prizes.* Describe the prizes, how many there are, how much each is worth and what happens to unclaimed prizes. In a game of chance, will you have a second drawing for unclaimed prizes?

- *Choosing of winners.* Tell the method you'll use—drawn at random, for example, or in the case of a skill contest, judged according to stated criteria. Also state how you'll notify winners that they've won, and how entrants can get a list of winners.

- *Odds of winning.* If only so many entries will be considered (say, the first 10,000), let entrants know that and tell them their odds of winning a prize. If you're not putting a cap on the number entries, then disclose that the odds of winning will depend on how many entries you get.

- *Disclaimers.* Computers are nowhere near perfect yet. Consider disclaiming any liability for problems caused by glitches in your server or hardware or software or for the loss or destruction of the entrant's data. Similarly, it's smart to disclaim liability if the entrant's system is harmed by downloading contest information from your website.

It can't hurt and may help to add, "Void where prohibited by law." This phrase can be useful if you inadvertently fail to comply with the technical requirements of some state's law.

If your rules are somewhat complicated, you might require participants to acknowledge they've read the rules and accept them perhaps by clicking "I Accept" before entering (see Chapter 6).

Make sure you register in states that require it. In a few states—Arizona, Florida, New York and Rhode Island—you have to file a registration statement in advance of your contest or sweepstakes and may also have to file a bond or set up a trust fund to assure that prizes will actually be awarded. Some states—for example, Arizona, Arkansas, California, Connecticut, Florida, Iowa, Minnesota, Maryland, New Mexico and Vermont—have laws regarding the use of entry fees or purchases for games of skill. Your lawyer can fill you in on these requirements.

F. The Importance of Good Customer Service

Attracting customers is just one ingredient of building a successful online business. You also need to keep your customers happy and loyal by offering them good service. Compared to a physical store where you can see your customers, get to know them and establish personal rapport, the Internet is anonymous and impersonal, so how you use your website to deal with customers becomes especially important. Here a few suggestions to consider:

- Give visitors multiple ways to communicate with you and place orders. You can provide an email address, a phone number and a fax number so people can get through to you, whichever way is most convenient. And, while an amazing number of websites neglect to do so, we recommend that you post a regular mailing address for those who prefer to contact you the old-fashioned way or just want to know where you're located.

- Answer all queries promptly, whether they arrive by email or other means. This is a great way to interact with customers, learn their needs and personalize your service.

- Ask customers for permission to add them to your email database so you can send them information about new products and services, and offer them special deals. And make it clear that they can easily have their name removed if they decide not to receive further email from you.

- Acknowledge all orders promptly with a sincere thank you. It just takes a moment to send the email. And even if the process is automated, customers appreciate it.

- When customers ask for items you don't carry, steer them to another site or store that may have it. It's wonderful if customers see your site as a source of helpful and reliable information.

- If someone places an order and then cancels it, send a friendly note acknowledging the cancellation. Add, "Thank you for your interest in our website. We look forward to hearing from you again."

- Install enough phone lines to handle incoming calls. Talking to customers by phone may not be as good as face-to-face communication, but it comes close. No one wants to get a busy signal or be placed on hold indefinitely.

- Consider paying for return shipping, especially if the customer has a good reason for the return. And if the product was defective, send out a replacement even before the original item comes back to you.

- Give customers a choice of shipping methods. Some prefer speed and are willing to pay the extra cost. Others prefer to save money on the shipping.

- Post Frequently Asked Questions (FAQs) on your website. The more answers visitors have, the more likely you'll convert them to customers. ■

Accepting Credit Card Orders

According to *The Wall Street Journal,* an estimated 95% of Internet purchases are completed with a credit card. It makes sense when you consider some of the alternatives—for example, shipping COD or requiring payment in advance. You'd get mighty few customers willing to go along with anything other than credit card payments.

The obvious advantages of a credit card transaction are that you get paid quickly and you don't have to worry about collection problems. If a customer doesn't pay a credit card bill, it's up to the bank that issued the credit card to collect the bill or absorb the loss. But all of this comes at a price. For one thing, you must pay hefty fees to become and remain a credit card merchant. And when credit cards are used for online transactions, there's a lot more room for fraud than when they're used for in-person purchases.

No doubt, in coming years, technology will provide consumer-friendly online payment methods that reduce the chances of your business being defrauded. Several new systems—variously dubbed *digital cash, virtual escrow, digital wallets* and *virtual credit cards*—are in the drawing board or testing stages. No one can tell you which, if any, will become the system of choice for businesses and consumers. Until a better system replaces credit cards, you'll have to accept

them and do the best you can to keep your fees and your losses to a minimum.

If you already have a brick-and-mortar business and accept credit cards, much of the information in this chapter will be familiar to you. But even if you're used to accepting credit cards, you'll need to know some special things about using them in cyberspace.

Look into PayPal if you're going to handle only a few sales online. For a small fee, the folks at PayPal (http://www.paypal.com) can handle all the details of your getting paid, and you won't need to set up a credit card merchant account. PayPal accepts your customers' credit card payments and transfers the money to your bank account. The PayPal system was originally created to process consumer-to-consumer transactions for people using the eBay auction site. But PayPal now handles business transactions as well. The procedures are clunky for both merchants and customers compared to traditional credit card transactions, but some small Web-based businesses with modest sales may find PayPal suitable.

A. How Credit Cards Work, Online and Off

Handling credit cards is fairly straightforward when the customer is physically present. The customer—who has obtained a credit card from an *issuing bank*—hands you the card; you pass it through a terminal. Phone lines to a processing firm—the transaction clearinghouse—connect the terminal and within seconds, you get verification that the card is valid and that the customer has sufficient credit to cover the transaction. Later, the money is sent to the bank that has authorized you to accept credit card payments—the *merchant bank*. Transaction fees and charges are deducted from your merchant bank account. The charge is added to the customer's monthly bill. The mechanics of in-store transactions are surprisingly easy and smooth. It's also simple to prove, if necessary, that the customer actually made the purchase because you have a signed charge slip.

By contrast, when you do business online, the mechanics are more cumbersome—and avoiding fraud is more difficult. For one thing, you have no credit card to swipe through a terminal and no signature. So, you need something approximating a card swipe machine. You also need a way to verify the credit card number and the amount of credit available—and a means for the banking system to transfer funds into your merchant account. In e-commerce lingo, you need a *gateway* that links your website to the credit card processing network. In summary, the key links in the online credit-card chain are:

- **Issuing Bank.** This is the bank that issues the credit card to the customer.
- **Merchant Bank (sometimes called Acquiring Bank).** To accept Visa, MasterCard and many other credit cards (but not American Express or Discover), your business must open a *merchant account* through a *merchant bank*. Not all merchant banks support use of their services for online transactions.
- **Transaction Clearinghouse.** To collect money from a customer, you don't deal directly with the customer's issuing bank. Instead, you deal with an intermediary known as a *transaction processor* or *clearinghouse* that handles credit card transactions for your merchant bank. The transaction processor checks the validity of the customer's card and OKs (or rejects) the purchase.
- **Gateway.** For online purchases, the gateway is the method of connecting your online business to the transaction clearinghouse. You can have a company (a gateway service) provide this, or you can purchase gateway software on disk or in hardware that acts as the digital equivalent of the card-swipe machine used in a store. Gateways allow for real-time checking of the credit card information so that the customer knows, at the time of purchase, whether the transaction has been approved. (See Section B3.)

Thanks to this sophisticated process, when a customer pays by credit card, the money winds up in your merchant account in about two or three days. As noted, American Express and Discover don't use this merchant bank system; you need to deal with those companies directly.

The types of fees charged for online credit card transactions vary widely, as do the amounts. Your online business may have to pay the fees listed below:

Credit Card Fees

Application Fee. You pay a one-time fee to create your merchant credit card account. $200 to $800

Monthly Premium Charge. Some merchant banks charge a monthly fee. Others establish a minimum monthly fee; if your total discount fees (see below) don't equal the minimum monthly fee, you pay the difference. $25 to $100

Transaction (Processing) Fee. You pay the credit card company for processing each purchase $.15 to $.65 per transaction

Discount Fee. You pay the credit card company a percentage of the price of each purchase. 2.0% to 3.5% of each transaction

Monthly Gateway Fee. If you use a gateway service to transmit data to the transaction clearinghouse, you pay a monthly fee for that service. $20 to $40 a month

---

As you can see, the bank or credit card company takes a sizable cut of the sale price (in addition to the other fees).

EXAMPLE: ProtoBiz.com sells a $10 item online to a customer who pays by credit card. Because ProtoBiz has agreed to a $.40 transaction fee and a 3% discount fee, the bank takes $.70 [$.40 + (3% of $10) = $.70] and Protobiz gets $9.30. ProtoBiz is also responsible for paying monthly charges.

Call it discrimination if you like, but if you do business online, you'll pay more in credit cards fees than someone with just a brick-and-mortar business would pay. That's because credit card companies view e-commerce transactions as inherently more risky than their real-world counterparts because of the greater chance for fraud and other problems. To help cover these anticipated losses, the bank charges you a higher rate for online transactions.

In addition to the fees listed above, some banks require a holdback—a percentage of sales that's kept in reserve to cover *chargebacks* (discussed below). And you'll probably have to pay set-up charges to cover equipment, software and installation required for getting hooked up to the credit card system.

Credit Card Lingo

Authorization—Confirmation from the consumer's credit card company that the credit card is in good standing and the necessary funds are available for the transaction.

Settlement—A process in which funds from the consumer's credit card bank are transferred into your merchant bank account.

Return—The opposite of an authorization. Money is taken from your merchant bank account and credited to the consumer's credit card bank. This usually happens when the consumer returns goods to you.

Chargeback—Taking the money out of your account because of a disputed transaction. You may have to pay a fee of $15 to $25 to the merchant bank for each disputed transaction.

B. Setting Up Your Online Account

The process of setting up to accept credit cards online can take two to four weeks, so plan accordingly. Here are some suggestions on how to proceed.

1. Choosing a Transaction Clearinghouse

It's probably easiest to start by choosing your transaction clearinghouse, because your merchant bank will want to know which clearinghouse you'll be using. Two of the leading online clearinghouses are Signio (http://www.signio.com) and CyberCash (http://www.cybercash.com). If you haven't chosen a merchant bank, the clearinghouse can recommend some and also provide gateway software. Keep your website developer in the loop when preparing to start an account; the clearinghouse may want to know what type of scripting code is used at your website—a technical issue that your website developer can deal with. Some clearinghouses such as Authorize.Net (http://www.authorizenet.com) and Verisign (http://www.verisign.com) are known as ISOs (Independent Sales Organizations). ISOs manage the whole process for a merchant, helping to set up the merchant bank account and gateway.

2. Opening a Merchant Bank Account

You must enter into a written agreement with the merchant bank. Check it carefully and make sure that the fees are as agreed.

Look out for excessive *chargeback* fees—the money a bank takes out of your business account when a customer disputes a transaction. Disputes about online transactions can pop up in several ways. For example, a customer may order merchandise, get it and keep it—but dispute that it was ever received. Or a customer may have some other complaint about the transaction. Unfair as it may seem, a bank typically can take a chargeback in any situation in which the customer is dissatisfied. In a retail store, chargebacks are rare, accounting for a mere 0.14% of credit transactions; but at an online store it's 1.25% of transactions. In other words, chargebacks are nine times more frequent in online transactions than in traditional store transactions. For that reason, compare chargeback rates at merchant banks before signing with a merchant bank. (See *Comparison Shop Before Picking Your Providers,* below.)

In addition, the merchant bank agreements will require that you comply with advertising restrictions set by the credit card companies—for example, how the images of the cards are displayed on the site. If you don't comply, you lose your merchant accounts.

3. Gateways

A gateway is a hardware or software process that connects your website to the transaction clearinghouse. You can buy gateway software, or sign up with a gateway service. If your business owns its own server (a computer that hosts your website), you can probably get along with gateway software. But most small businesses—whether or not they own

their own servers—will find it much more convenient to sign up with a gateway service such as that offered by CyberCash (http://www.cybercash.com). Online demos at the CyberCash site offer a hands-on preview of how the service works.

Comparison Shop Before Picking Your Providers

Obviously, fees can eat into your profits, so you need to check them thoroughly before you sign up to be a credit card merchant. You can do comparison shopping on the web at MerchantWorkz (http://www.merchantworkz.com), a site that provides clearinghouse and merchant bank fees, merchant bank profiles and advice on gateways and the other necessary elements for setting up an online credit card account.

C. Minimizing Fraud

Credit card fraud can occur in a couple of ways. Sometimes, a customer will intentionally rip you off. Other times, the credit-card holder is also a victim because the card has been stolen. Either way, if there's a loss in an online credit card transaction, it's you, the merchant, who winds up losing money.

EXAMPLE: A customer calling herself Jane Jones orders a $500 painting from ProtoBiz.com and charges it to a Visa credit card. ProtoBiz's owner checks with Visa which verifies that there is a Jane Jones with the specified credit card number. ProtoBiz ships the painting to the address that Jane designated. A few days later, Merchant Bank where ProtoBiz has its merchant account, deposits $485 ($500 less a $15 discount fee) into ProtoBiz's bank account. Merchant Bank then bills Jane. Jane calls Merchant Bank and says, "I never ordered a painting. Take the charge off my credit card account." Unfortunately, ProtoBiz can't prove that Jane did order the painting because it doesn't have her signature on a charge slip and it can't prove that she received the painting because her signature isn't on the delivery slip and the painting wasn't sent to her address. Merchant Bank takes $485 out of ProtoBiz's account.

In our example, Jane may have deliberately defrauded the merchant, or someone may have stolen Jane's credit card or just gotten hold of the credit card information.

Gateway software and services can help keep you from being a victim of credit-card fraud. The cost in software or services is usually money well spent. For example, the software or service can do a comparison to make sure that the shipping address is the same as the customer's billing address. If not, you're given a chance to decide whether you want to check further before completing the transaction.

You may want to speak to the customer by phone to make sure that everything's on the up and up before you ship out the merchandise. Of course, you'll need to exercise some judgment to determine if you're speaking to the true card owner and if you can later establish that that's who placed the order. Sometimes it's a tough judgment call because there are perfectly valid reasons why a customer wants to have an order shipped to an address other than the billing address. For example, the merchandise being shipped may be a gift. Or the billing address may be the customer's home and the customer may prefer to receive the product at work where he or she will be present to receive it during normal delivery hours.

Your gateway software or transaction clearinghouse can also provide additional fraud protection services. Some popular software add-ons include:

- **Fraud Protection.** This system lets you rate the chances that a particular transaction will be fraudulent based on criteria that you select. If you think a transaction is flagged as especially risky, you can seek further information from the customer or reject the transaction entirely.

- **AVS.** This system (short for Address Verification Service) takes the first five numbers of the street address and the ZIP code information from the customer's stated billing address and compares that data to the billing address the card issuer has. You're told if there's a good match. If not, you can decide to reject the sale.

- **CIC.** Every credit card has a Card Identification Code, a three- or four-digit number that's printed on the credit card in addition to the 16-digit embossed number. You can minimize fraud by including a feature that checks this number, since only someone who actually has the card in hand will know the number. Some companies call the number a CVV2, CVC2 or CID.

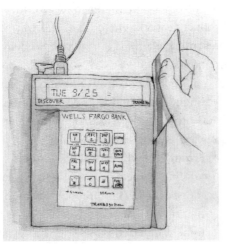

Some merchandise lends itself to fraud. Criminals tend to order items that they can easily turn into cash, such as jewelry or sound systems. And gift certificates are especially attractive to them since they can be sold at a discounted price. Be extra vigilant if you deal in such items. You're also at greater risk of fraud if you sell digital goods or site memberships. Here, the digital data are simply downloaded into the customer's computer. No street address is required for delivery.

When you take orders online, your form should, at a minimum, require the customer to enter the:

- type of card (for example, Visa)
- card number
- name on card
- expiration date
- billing address.

It can also be useful to ask for the name of the bank that issued the card. And you might also ask for a phone number so you can call the customer if something seems fishy.

Here are a few more security tips to round out those given out by the credit card issuers:

- Be extra careful in processing an order from a new customer—especially if the customer places a large order and asks for overnight delivery.

- Proceed cautiously if someone orders a large quantity of children's or teenagers' merchandise. It may be that a child or teenager has borrowed a parent's credit card.
- Consider rejecting purchases when a bank in a foreign country has issued the credit card. This may seem harsh, but foreign credit cards are reported to have a higher fraud rate than those issued by U.S. banks.
- When you ship merchandise, choose a shipment method that requires the card owner to sign a receipt. This route adds some expense to transactions but you'll know whether or not the shipment arrived.

No doubt, more secure methods will be developed. For example, someday there may be devices that can scan a cardholder's retina or fingerprints to verify that you're dealing with the actual card owner. With that kind of positive identification, an online credit-card transaction would become about as reliable as one taking place in a store. Meanwhile, the best you can do is keep up to date on what kind of software and related technology is on the market for credit card transactions.

Are you using a secure server?

Most Web hosting services can connect you to a secure server—although they may charge you a bit more. It's well worth it. You and your customers will enjoy greater peace of mind. Otherwise, customers will be (rightly) worried about whether their credit card information will fall into the wrong hands.

In Chapter 6, Section E1, we suggest that you post a policy offering customers up to $50 if a customer is charged for fraudulent purchases. ■

CHAPTER

11

After the Sale:
Shipping, Taxes and Refunds

t's always gratifying when a customer purchases an item at your website, but your job doesn't end when you've emptied the customer's shopping cart. Your Web business must still deal with shipping, sales tax and the occasional refund. If you've never run a mail order operation, you need to learn about federal and state laws that govern these aspects of your online business.

This book focuses on U.S. law. Different rules may apply to international transactions. If you're selling to people in other countries, you're likely to come within the jurisdiction of their countries' laws. You could easily violate those laws without realizing it. For example, German law prohibits the use of product comparisons in advertising—and some Scandinavian countries prohibit ads directed at children. So if you plan to transact business with customers in other countries, you'll need to consult a lawyer familiar with laws abroad.

A. Shipping

If you take orders online, you must follow the shipping and refund rules of the Federal Trade Commission's Mail or Telephone Order Merchandise Rule. Despite its name, the rule applies to online sales as well as mail and phone orders.

Many websites tell customers when they can expect orders to be shipped. For example, you may say, "all orders shipped the next day" or "generally shipped within three days." If you give a shipping time frame on your website, you must state it clearly, post it prominently and have a good reason to believe you can meet it.

If you say nothing about when you ship orders, you must have a reasonable basis for believing that you can ship the product within 30 days of taking the order.

If you can't ship within the time promised on your website or within the 30 days required by the FTC, you must:

- notify the customer of the delay (email is OK)
- provide a revised shipment date, and
- explain that the order can be cancelled for a full and prompt refund.

EXAMPLE: ProtoBiz.com receives an online order from Julie for a patio table and four chairs. The ProtoBiz website doesn't mention a delivery date, but the company believes it can easily ship the table and chairs within 30 days because its supplier has almost always been able to fill orders in a week to ten days. Later, ProtoBiz learns that the supplier is shutting down for vacation, and that the table and chairs can't be shipped to Julie for six weeks. ProtoBiz promptly sends Julie an email message informing her of the delay and telling her she can cancel and get a prompt refund. Julie replies that she'd like to wait for the chairs.

If you don't hear back from the customer, but are confident you can deliver the merchandise within 30 days of notification, you can treat the customer's silence as agreement. But for longer or indefinite delays and for second and subsequent delays, you need the customer's consent. If you don't get it, you have to refund the customer's money without being asked. And, as you might expect, if you discover that you'll never be able to fill the order, you must promptly send a refund.

EXAMPLE: ProtoBiz.com discovers that the manufacturer of the table and chairs that Julie ordered has gone out of business and there's no way to get the merchandise. ProtoBiz promptly cancels Julie's order, informs her of the cancellation and credits her Visa card account for her payment.

Finally, if there's going to be a shipping delay and you don't want to seek the customer's consent, you can simply cancel the order. If you decide to cancel, you must promptly notify the customer and refund the payment. We don't recommend this option, however. For one thing, it will probably disappoint and irri-

tate the customer. For another, you may be walking away from a possible sale needlessly, since the customer, if given chance, may go along with the delay.

If you take an order by phone, you can satisfy the FTC's requirements by telling the customer of the delay during the conversation. It's a bit more complicated, however, when a customer orders online. Legally, the online order is complete when the customer clicks it along to you. So you'll have to notify the customer of the delay by email, phone, fax or regular mail. When you notify the customer—by whatever means—it's a prudent practice to keep a record of how you gave the notice, when you gave it and how the customer responded.

Below is an example of a first delay notice. You can use this format when the date you insert is 30 days or less later than the original promised time.

The notices provided below may be found on the CD-ROM at the back of the book.

NOTICE OF DELAY: FIRST NOTICE

We're sorry, but we won't be able to ship you the table and four chairs you ordered until _____, 20XX. If you don't want to wait, you may cancel your order and receive a prompt refund by calling our toll-free number, 800-555-1234. If we don't hear from you before we ship the merchandise, we'll assume that you still want us to ship your order. Remember, if you want the merchandise, you don't have to call us.

We apologize for the delay.

If your first delay notice gives a revised shipment date more than 30 days from the promised date or you don't know when you'll be able to ship, you must tell your customers that if they don't respond, you'll cancel the order 30 days after you originally promised to deliver the goods. Below is an example of a notice you might use if don't have a new shipping date.

NOTICE OF DELAY:
NO NEW SHIPPING DATE

Because our supplier has unexpectedly closed down for vacation for three weeks, we can't ship you the table and four chairs you ordered. We don't know when we'll be able to ship this merchandise. If you don't want to wait, you may cancel your order and receive a prompt refund by calling our toll-free number, 800-555-1234.

If we don't hear from you and we haven't shipped by _____, 20XX, your order will be canceled automatically and your money will be refunded.

If you don't want your order automatically canceled on _____, 20XX, you may request that we keep your order and fill it later. In that case, you can still cancel the order at any time before we ship it to you. You may use our toll-free number, 800-555-1234, either to request that we fill your order later or to cancel it.

We apologize for the delay.

Non-compliance can be expensive. In 2001, the FTC sued seven Internet retailers in federal court for filling holidays orders too late. At issue was the retailers' failure to promptly give consumers the choice of consenting to a shipping delay or canceling their orders and getting a quick refund. The retailers agreed to settle for $1.5 million in fines. You can find more about these cases and other information about the federal rules that govern mail, phone and online orders at the Federal Trade Commission website at http://www.ftc.gov.

B. Sales Tax

Taxation of Internet transactions is a hot political topic. For now, Congress has placed a moratorium on any new federal Internet taxes while the issue is investigated and debated. But if you're engaged in e-commerce, you may still be obligated to collect and pay state and local sales taxes. State and local rules vary widely as to what items are subject to the tax and what the tax rate is.

As matters now stand, you only have to collect tax on online transactions when the customer is in a state or city where your business has a substantial physical presence. If the customer is anywhere else, you're not required to collect sales tax. So, for the majority of your Internet customers, that means tax-free purchasing.

EXAMPLE: ProtoBiz.com has its management offices in California, three stores in Oregon and a warehouse in Washington. It must collect and pay state sales tax on sales to people and businesses located in those three states. It can ignore the sales tax when completing a sale to someone living in New York.

If you have facilities in several states, your life will be more complicated (see "How the Big Players Avoid Sales Tax," below). You'll have to check with the revenue department in each state to learn the applicable tax rules or consult a knowledgeable tax lawyer or CPA. Also, you might look into software that helps process multi-state sales taxes. Be aware that because some cities and counties also impose a sales tax, compliance can be quite complex.

It's difficult to predict the staying power of the current rules that make many Internet purchases tax-free. As this book goes to press (December, 2001), President Bush had signed into law an extension of the Internet sales tax ban for two years. To stay current with Internet tax law, check out EcommerceTax.com (http://www.ecommercetax.com).

How the Big Players Avoid Sales Tax

Many big retailers with local stores can sell their products tax-free to a large segment of their Internet customers. They can do this because they've created separate affiliates to handle Internet business. For example, the Barnes & Noble you buy a book from online is a different company from Barnes & Noble at the mall. If the online Barnes & Noble doesn't have a physical presence in your state, no sales tax is charged for your online purchases.

C. Your Refund Policy

The law on refunds—in the real and cyber worlds—is clear. Once a sale is complete, you don't have to give refunds. This is based on traditional contract law, which treats a sale as a completed contract. The only exceptions are if:

- there's been a significant breach of the contract—for example, the goods or services you sold were seriously flawed, or
- an agreement between your business and the customer allows the customer to cancel the sale and get a refund.

So a customer who buys a product from you doesn't have the legal right to cancel the contract later and automatically get a refund. By the same token, if you discover that you could have charged a higher price, you can't cancel the sale either.

So much for the legalities. In real life, many online businesses give customers the option of returning merchandise for either a cash refund or at least a credit toward another online purchase. Sometimes businesses impose conditions. For example, the customer must return the merchandise within a certain number of days, the merchandise must be unused or the customer must submit a receipt or other proof of purchase.

A liberal refund policy can give your customers confidence in your business and can be an effective marketing technique. By definition, online customers can't examine the merchandise before the sale. Few will buy from you if there's no chance of a refund. Whatever you decide to do about a customer recourse policy, word your rules as positively as possible.

Post your return and refund policy prominently on your site. State law may require it, and it's a good practice whether or not it's the law in your state. California law (Cal. Civ. Code § 1723) even specifies where you must post your policy. It must appear on:

- the first screen on your site
- the screen where you first offer goods or services for sale
- the screen where a buyer places an order, or
- the screen where the buyer enters payment information, such as a credit card number. ■

Respecting Your Customers' Privacy

Internet businesses have access to more consumer information than was ever available in the strictly brick-and-mortar world. That's because tracking software and database technology can follow the Internet surfing habits of every Web user and record information about their preferences and buying history. To replicate that information offline, you'd have to hire private investigators to follow all your customers before they entered the store, while they shopped and after they went home.

At the simplest level, your Web business can learn what pages someone visits on your website. If the visitor buys something, you'll get a name, address and credit card information. With a little more sophistication, you can also track where the visitor was on the Internet just before and after using your site. You can use this information to help target your advertising, and you can sell the information to other businesses, too.

But along with this ease in collecting data has come a heightened concern among online shoppers about protecting their personal information. With the exception of a federal law regulating sites that attract children under 13 years of age (see Section D, below), few laws protect the privacy of people using the Internet. One way to make visitors feel more comfortable about becoming customers at your site is to display and follow a clear privacy policy that states how you gather and use information. These days, almost all reputable e-commerce sites have a good privacy policy—and you should too.

If you're not keeping or selling personal information about your customers, you can get by just posting a simple, reassuring privacy policy. In other situations, however, you'll want a more extensive posting.

Numerous companies can show you how to harvest data about site visitors. These companies can provide software and other technical assistance that lets you seize the marketing opportunities this data affords. For an idea of the kinds of services that are available, look at http://www.webtrends.com.

We Have Recommendations for *You!*

One of the most visible examples of targeted marketing can be seen on the Amazon.com site. Amazon uses buying histories to pitch books to individual customers when they return to the site. In its most benign form, this is similar to having the local book merchant who knowing your reading habits, shows you a new arrival that you might like. But on the Internet, there's considerable resistance to having a company know so much about a particular consumer. This is sometimes tempered by the ridiculous nature of the results—for example, if you've bought a gardening book as a gift for your father a baby book for a pregnant friend, and a mystery for yourself, Amazon doesn't really know much about you after all.

A. The Information You Gather

The information you collect at your website may or may not identify individuals, and it may come to you either because individuals volunteer it or because you collect it automatically.

1. Generic vs. Specific Information

Information gathered on the Internet is divided into two broad categories: general information which does not identify individual users and specific information which does. Site visitors don't care how you collect and use general information. They won't be concerned, for example, if a health information website, looking for sponsorship by a drug company, reveals that 2,000 people a day visit the site to learn about toenail fungus. But users *will* become uneasy if that same health website decides to sell a drug company the names and email addresses of the people who sought information on that topic. That's why your privacy policy should say whether you collect information about specific identifiable individuals and, if you do, how you use that information. And you should cover this topic whether the customer actively gives you information or you acquire it in ways the customer doesn't know about.

2. Information Customers Volunteer

The most common way you'll gather information from your customers is the old-fashioned way, by asking them. Many websites ask customers to fill out registration forms or ask for personal information when a customer buys a product or service. Similarly, if you run a contest, entrants may have to submit personal information. The information you gather can be quite extensive: name, address, phone number and email addresses are just the beginning. You may wind up with information about a visitor's clothing size, tastes in music, hobbies, age or employment.

Laws in the United States don't dictate what you can and can't do with this information. You can use it to advertise additional goods or services to the customers. And you're free to share or sell the information to others. This is true whether the information is generic or can be used to identify specific people. (With a site that targets or attracts children, federal law requires posting a privacy policy. See Section D, below.)

But consumers, particularly Internet consumers, are becoming savvy about protecting their private information on the Internet. So, even though the law doesn't require it, it's a good idea to give consumers a choice about what you do with information they provide you. (If you don't, many will decline to provide it at all.)

An *opt-in* policy allows consumers to read a privacy policy and choose whether or not to allow use of their personal information. With an *opt-out* policy, a company gathers and uses information from a consumer until that person asks it to stop.

This may seem like just a semantic quibble, but the results can be dramatically different depending on which route you follow. Few consumers actually bother to opt out, which allows a company to sell or share their information. But given the opportunity to opt in and allow sharing of information, many customers choose not to have their information shared. So with an opt-out system, you'll end up with more data on your customers. But customers and customer-friendly website owners prefer the opt-in route, which is more respectful of the customer's privacy.

3. Information You Gather Automatically

There are several ways that websites can gather information without a customer knowing. The best-known method is through the use of *cookies*. A cookie is a file that's created on the computer of a site visitor. It stores information about pages visited and purchases made. When the customer returns, a business can read the information about previous visits and direct the customer to products or services of potential interest. Creating cookies and reading them, later, are accomplished by software that is installed as part of your website. A developer can explain the principles and there are articles available on the Internet that describe the process".

Internet advertising companies also use cookies. When a user reaches a Web page that has an ad on it, the advertising company can put a cookie on a computer hard drive, even if the website itself chooses not to use cookies. Whenever a visitor is online, the cookie can send information back to the ad firm on what parts of the site the person is exploring.

Another way to gather potentially valuable information is through recording the *browsing patterns* of an Internet user. This can usually only be done by the online service that a person joins to obtain access to the Internet. This information is commercially valuable because direct marketers can use it to target email spam campaigns.

B. Privacy Regulation

Surprisingly, despite all the concerns about privacy on the Web, there are very few legal restraints on how an e-commerce business can handle personal information. If you address your site to customers in the United States and you don't focus on children younger than 13 or gather personal information from these youngsters, you're pretty much free of any governmental regulation.

Follow the laws. To keep abreast of changes in the laws regulating Internet privacy, visit http://www.privacyrights.org, a consumer-oriented website that closely watches privacy issues and regulations.

1. Federal

The federal government doesn't regulate the use of consumer information gathered from the Web, except when it comes to children. However, once a business posts a privacy policy, it must abide by it or risk the attention of the Federal Trade Commission (FTC). Violations of voluntary privacy policies are considered a type of deceptive business practice.

It's not clear whether new privacy regulations will be enacted. In October, 2001, the Federal Trade Commission announced that the agency will not seek stronger consumer privacy laws. However, Congress is considering several bills that would regulate personal information gathered in e-commerce. Consumer groups, armed with numerous complaints about misuse of personal information, are pushing for federal laws that would limit the use of personal information and force businesses to tell visitors what they do with that information.

2. State

State legislatures have been reluctant to enact laws addressing the privacy of consumer information gathered on the Web, perhaps believing that such regulation would make more sense at the national level. Whatever the reason, proposals for such laws have been floated in several states, but haven't resulted in new laws.

However, California has opened the door by creating an Office of Privacy Protection. Recommendations from that agency may lead to laws or regulations in that state that will affect personally identifiable information in e-commerce. But for now, if you post a privacy policy as recommended in this chapter, especially if consumers can opt out of your plan to share or sell information, it's highly unlikely that you'll get tripped up by any state privacy laws anywhere in the United States.

3. European

It would be nearly impossible for a small business to keep track of privacy policies in every country around the world. And, even if you could, it would be prohibitively expensive. That's one reason this book focuses on doing business in the United States. But if you do any business with European customers, you should know about the European Union's privacy policy.

Countries of the European Union

Austria	Italy
Belgium	Luxembourg
Denmark	Netherlands
Finland	Portugal
France	Spain
Germany	Sweden
Greece	United Kingdom
Ireland	

The 15 countries of the EU are a potentially huge market for your goods and services. But, unlike the United States, the EU has an extensive set of privacy laws and regulations called the Directive on Data Protection. It controls online privacy for the entire EU.

The EU Directive is designed to protect information relating to an *identified* or *identifiable* person. An identifiable person, according to the EU, is one who can be identified, directly or indirectly, through an identification number, or factors specific to his or her physical, physiological, mental, economic, cultural or social identity.

The requirements of the EU Directive (summarized below) are complex and go beyond what most companies in the U.S. are currently doing. Officials of the United States and the EU are trying to reach agreement on a simple system to help U.S. businesses comply with the European standards. While those arrangements are being worked out, it's unlikely that the EU would fine a small U.S. company for failing to comply with the EU Directive. But there's a way you can protect your business now from any risk of a problem. The U.S. Department of Commerce has a "safe harbor" program that you can join; it will protect you from any enforcement action by the EU. For a comprehensive explanation of the EU Directive, go to the site maintained by the U.S. Department of Commerce at http://www.export.gov/safeharbor. Then, click Safe Harbor Workbook.

Keep in mind that you need to consider the safe harbor program only if you expect to do business with customers in EU nations. So if you don't expect to solicit business in any EU nations or if your business with EU citizens is rare or trivial—for example, less than 1% of your sales—you don't need to worry about meeting the requirements.

Here are the key requirements of the EU Directive:

- **Data Quality.** You must handle personal information fairly and lawfully. For example, you must let people know that you're collecting personal information and how you propose to use it. You must use the information only for the purposes you've listed, and must not collect more data than you need for that purpose. For example, if someone provides informa-

tion to get phone service, the information shouldn't be used to target the person for information about vacation trips.

- **Data Processing.** Basically, before you process information (collect it for sharing or sale, for example) you need to get the consent of the person giving you the information. You also have to let people know whether or not they have the right to see the information you're collecting and to correct anything that's not accurate. And you've got to say what types of businesses are going to receive the data.

- **Sensitive Data.** For the most part, unless you have explicit consent, you can't collect sensitive data at all. Sensitive data is defined as information about racial or ethnic origins, political or religious beliefs, or health or sex life.

- **Security.** You need to take appropriate steps to protect data from loss, alteration or unauthorized use.

There's a simple way to avoid EU privacy policies. If you don't want to spend the time or effort to create a privacy policy acceptable to EU countries, you should aim your website solely at U.S. customers. See Chapter 8,Section D, for suggestions on how to do that.

C. Putting Together a Privacy Policy

If you want visitors and customers to give you personal information you should be willing to give them a clearly stated and reasonable explanation of how you're going to use and protect that information. Fortunately, crafting a good privacy policy isn't difficult. This section shows you how.

1. Should You Have a Privacy Policy?

Even though there's no law currently requiring a privacy policy for general audience sites, there are several good reasons to establish reasonable privacy policies and let people know what they are:

- *It will help you build better relationships with customers and prospective customers*. Visitors to your website are more likely to order from you and use your services if they know what use you'll make of the information they give you. If your privacy policies are reasonable, customers will be reassured and feel more confident in doing business with you.
- *It will help you compete against other online businesses*. Virtually all websites that customers trust and return to have privacy policies in place. Not having a posted policy may brand your site as amateurish, if not suspect.

- *It may enable you to do business with European customers*. If you do business with people in Europe, you'll need a posted privacy policy to comply with European Union privacy laws.
- *It will let you hit the ground running if and when Congress adopts e-commerce privacy standards*. Rather than starting from scratch, you'll just have to tinker a bit with your privacy practices if they don't quite meet the new legal standards. You won't have to scurry around to create a privacy policy under the pressure of a legal deadline.

Despite all these good reasons for having a privacy policy, there's a downside you should consider. As noted in Section B, if you post a privacy policy but fail to follow it, the FTC or a state agency may sue you, claiming that you engaged in a deceptive business practice.

EXAMPLE: ProtoBiz posts a privacy policy stating: "We will never disclose your personal information to outsiders without your consent." Six months later, ProtoBiz rents its customer database to a company that aggressively markets insurance policies. Several ProtoBiz customers receive solicitations from the insurance company and figure out that the company received personal information from ProtoBiz. The Federal Trade Commission takes action against ProtoBiz for deception. ProtoBiz has to pay some legal costs and publicly apologize for its error.

Your Privacy Policy—Selling and Renting Customer Information

It is not against the law to sell or rent customer information. However, it is a violation of law to promise customers you won't sell the information and then later break that promise. (In 2001, for example, the FTC fined DirectWeb $15,000 for selling customer information after promising that it would not do so.) Keep in mind that even if you do not plan to sell or rent the information, your promise to preserve privacy can create a problem for you if your company runs into financial problems and you wish to sell the lists as an asset of your business. Companies such as eToys and Living.com found this out when they attempted to sort out bankruptcy filings in 2001. (This is not to say that DirectWeb, eToys and Living.com could not have changed their policies—they could—but these changes would not have been retroactive.) In short, if you are not sure about what you will do with customer information, do not promise you won't sell or rent the information.

The FTC or a state agency is much more likely to pursue a large company than a small one for this type of violation, and probably will act only in an aggravated case. Whether or not consumers themselves have a right to sue you for this kind of deception is unclear. Still, if you post a privacy policy and want to stay out of trouble, you should do what you say you'll do.

2. Elements of a Good Privacy Policy

A well-crafted privacy policy should explain:

- What types of personally identifiable information you collect on your website.
- How you collect this information—for example, through order forms.
- How you use the information.
- With whom you may share the information.
- The choices a visitor has regarding personal information—for example, requesting that it be deleted or that it not be used for marketing.
- The security procedures you use to protect the information.
- Whether a visitor who declines to provide requested information will be locked out of certain parts of your website.
- How a visitor can correct inaccurate information.
- How a visitor can find out if you change your policy.
- How a visitor can contact your business—by phone, fax, email and regular mail.

3. Where to Start

This section outlines three ways to go about creating your own privacy policy. Whichever you use, you'll need to make sure you tailor your policy to the specifics of your website. None of the methods is superior to the others, so review each of them and decide which works best for you.

a. Look to Your Favorite Websites for Guidance

A good starting point for writing your own privacy policy is to check some commercial websites you've dealt with and that you feel have treated you well. After looking at several sites, you'll probably notice that there's a wide variation in the language used. Some will be stilted and legalistic. Others will be clear and direct, using plain English—which is how you'd like your privacy policy to turn out. With clear language, customers will know exactly where they stand. It's friendlier. Your privacy notice can do more than just lay out the rules you'll be following. It can also let customers know that your business is approachable and sincerely interested in its customers.

b. Use TRUSTe's Privacy Policy Wizard

Another method of preparing privacy rules is to use an online privacy service to help write your policy. At http://www.truste.com/wizard, you'll find a questionnaire that you can complete in less than five minutes. Then, with a few more clicks, you'll have a respectable privacy policy for your site—though you'll want to fine-tune it to meet your specific needs. The questionnaire and automated policy preparation are free. While at the site, learn about the services that TRUSTe offers.

A Seal of Approval

TRUSTe (http://www.truste.com) is a prominent private organization that will certify that your privacy policies and practices meet consumer-friendly standards. Another well-respected organization offering similar services is the venerable Better Business Bureau (http://www.bbbonline.org). If your privacy policy meets their standards and you're careful to comply with the policy, you can post the organization's logo on your site. This helps reassure visitors that you're on the up and up, and that their personal information is in good hands. Of course, organizations that certify and monitor you expect to be paid for their services, but the fees, which are tied to a company's income, are quite modest.

---

c.   Use Our Sample Form

You can draft your privacy policy using the sample form in Section C4, below. As with the TRUSTe form (or any other privacy policy form, for that matter) you'll need to review it carefully and make the changes you need to fit your business.

4.   A Sample Privacy Policy

What goes into a privacy policy depends on many things, including the kind of business you're running and the kind of relationship you'd like to establish with your customers. Our sample policy is customer-friendly, written in plain, non-legalistic language. For a sample policy for a website that caters to children under 13, see Section D.

Our Privacy Policy

ProtoBiz is committed to protecting your privacy. We use the information we collect about you to process orders and to personalize your experience at our website. This privacy statement explains how we gather information and how we protect your privacy.

Your consent

By using our website, you consent to the collection and use of this information by ProtoBiz.

The information that ProtoBiz collects

Ordering Online. When you order, we need to know your name, email address, mailing address, credit card number and expiration date. This allows us to process and fulfill your order and to notify you of your order status.

Promotions, Online Surveys & Announcements. If you decide to participate in an online survey, subscribe to an email list, enter a contest or use one of our other promotional features, we may ask for your name, address, email address and other pertinent information to administer the contest, tabulate survey results or add you to subscriber lists.

Browsing. We may use "cookies" to help us process your order and to customize information that we may present to you. A cookie is a small text file that does not personally identify users, although it does identify a user's computer. Cookies do not pose a threat to your computer, and they do not contain viruses. Most Web browsers automatically accept cookies, but you can change this feature in your browser.

How ProtoBiz protects your information

When you place an order, we use a secure server to protect your sensitive information. The secure server software encrypts all information you input before it is sent to us. Your information is used only to process and send orders, bill credit cards and to contact you when necessary.

How we use information you supply in online order forms and registration

ProtoBiz does not sell or rent customer lists. ProtoBiz may partner with other similar companies to offer special services to our customers, in which case we will share the names and email addresses of our customers with those partners, but we will not release any other information to them about individuals.

Of course, ProtoBiz may disclose personal information if legally required to do so or if necessary to comply with legal process served on ProtoBiz, to protect ProtoBiz rights or property or to take emergency action to protect the personal safety of users of the ProtoBiz website or the public.

[Comment: If you do plan to rent your customer list, you can change the first sentence of this paragraph to read as follows: ProtoBiz sometimes rents its customer list (names and addresses only) to companies that offer products and services we think our customers may be interested in.]

Links to other sites

The ProtoBiz website includes links to other sites we think you might be interested in. ProtoBiz is not responsible for the privacy practices or the content of such sites. Be aware of where you are at all times!

Removing your information

If you give ProtoBiz your contact information over this website, and you wish to have your name removed from ProtoBiz's database, please send us an email to privacy@protobiz.com, and we will remove your name.

Changes to our privacy policy

If we change our privacy policy, we will post the changes on this page.

Contacting us

ProtoBiz welcomes your questions and comments about privacy. You can reach us in any of the following ways:

Email: _____

Fax: _____

Regular mail: _____

Phone: _____

5. Where to Post Your Privacy Policy

Make your privacy policy easy to find. A single click should take the customer from your home page to the privacy notice. It should also be readily accessible from any page where the customer is asked to give personal information. All the privacy information should be together in a single document—not scattered around in different places on your website.

D. Protecting Children's Privacy

Children under 13 years old have special privacy protection on the Internet. A Web business that deals with them must follow specific rules on how to use their personal information—or face stiff fines. The rules are contained in the federal Children's Online Privacy Protection Act (COPPA), which is enforced by the Federal Trade Commission. Complying with COPPA can be difficult because the rules are complex and are not always clear.

The law is an attempt to keep businesses from using the Internet unfairly to get young children to buy goods and services. The theory is that because kids are curious and trusting, they may give up more personal information than is prudent. Consequently, COPPA tries to give parents a say about the information their children give out.

COPPA is concerned only with collection of *individually identifiable information* from a child under 13—information that would let someone identify or contact the child. Such information, for example, might consist of the child's full name, home address, email address or phone number. The law also covers other types of information—such as hobbies, interests and information collected through cookies or other tracking mechanisms—when they're tied to individually identifiable information. If you don't collect individually identifiable information about people visiting your site, you're free and clear of COPPA.

The FTC Flexes Its Muscle

In April 2001, the FTC signed settlement agreements with three websites that collected personally identifying information from children under 13 without getting parental consent. The websites agreed to pay a total of $100,000 in civil penalties.

In addition, the companies agreed to delete all the personal information they collected in violation of COPPA and to link their sites to http://www.ftc.gov/kidzprivacy, where the FTC provides information to consumers about the statute.

1. Sites Covered by Special Federal Rules

COPPA regulates websites under two circumstances:

- your site is directed at children under 13, or
- you know that children under 13 are visiting your site.

But the rules that help you decide whether your site fits into these categories are vague.

a. Sites Directed at Children

If your site is directed at children under 13 and you collect personal information from those children, you must follow the COPPA rules for handling the information you gather. The FTC rules don't define what constitutes a site "directed at children," but they do say that a site may fit that description if it:

- offers subject matter of interest to kids
- contains visual or audio content designed to appeal to kids
- uses young models
- uses animated characters or other child-oriented features
- presents online ads that are directed to children, or
- actually does draw an abundance of children as visitors.

If you have a site that's directed at children, the FTC assumes that each person from whom you collect information is under the age of 13. Of course, that assumption isn't always correct. But if the FTC looks into your privacy practices, it's up to you to show that the COPPA privacy rules don't apply in your dealings with a specific individual. You'll need to establish that the person is 13 or older, or at least that you had good reason to think so—for example, the person used a credit card to complete a purchase.

b. Sites That Attract Children

Even if your site is a general-audience site not directed at children younger than 13, it's possible that you must follow the COPPA rules. If you know that you're collecting information from people under 13 years old, you must follow COPPA rules with regard to their information. How can you know if you're collecting information from these minors? Certainly, if you ask for people's ages or birth dates, you'll know. The same is true if people simply volunteer their age. But in most other cases, you probably won't have a clue about how old someone is. In this situation, if the FTC starts investigating your privacy practices, no one knows how it will go about establishing your knowledge of a person's age.

If you have a general-audience site and you learn that a child under 13 has given you personal information, you may want to simply delete that information—it's simpler than meeting COPPA requirements.

2. Complying With Federal Law

If you decide your website must meet COPPA requirements, you must:

- post your privacy policy
- get parental consent before you collect personal information (in most cases)
- get new consent for policy changes before you collect personal information (in most cases)
- let parents review personal information you collect from their children, and
- let parents revoke their consent, and delete information you collected.

a. When You Don't Need Prior Consent

In a few cases, you don't need a parent's consent before you can collect and use a child's personal information. For example, you don't need consent when you:

- Obtain a child's or parent's email address so you know where to send a privacy notice to ask for required consent.
- Get an email address to respond to a *one-time* request from a child and then delete it. This might happen, for example, if a child asked you for more information about a contest you were running.
- Get an email address to respond more than once to a specific request—say

for a subscription to a newsletter. Here, you must notify the parent that you're communicating regularly with the child. You must give the parent the opportunity to stop the communication before you send a second communication to the child.

Below is a sample notice for when you plan to communicate more than once with a minor.

SAMPLE NOTICE TO PARENT

To the parent of

_____:

Your child, _____, has requested that we send a subscription to protobiz.com's monthly newsletter, *ProtoBuzz*. We have started the subscription and have sent your child the first issue by email at the following address:

_____.

You can inform us now—or at any future time—that you want us to stop the subscription. Just email us at _____ giving us your name, your child's name and your child's email address. We will promptly comply with your instructions.

Sincerely,

ProtoBiz

The FTC rules also let you collect and use a child's personal information without a parent's prior consent to protect the safety of a child using your site. Unfortunately, the FTC doesn't give any examples of what this means, but presumably it would be OK to get a child's name and give it to the police if you felt the child were in danger. In that case, you'd have to let the parent know what you've done, and the parent could then prevent further use of the information.

You're also allowed to collect a child's personal information to protect the security of your site or to respond to a law enforcement request, but you can't later use the information for any other purpose.

b. Signing Up With a Compliance Program

One method of complying with COPPA is to join a safe harbor program. The FTC has approved several privately run programs that meet COPPA standards. If your business participates in one of these programs and sticks to its guidelines, you'll be deemed to be complying with COPPA.

Look into the programs run by TRUSTe (http://www.truste.com), the Children's Advertising Review Unit, which is part of the Better Business Bureau (http://www.bbb.org) and the Entertainment Software Rating Board (http://www.esrb.org). Others may be added to the FTC list, so check the FTC site (http://www.ftc.gov).

Another benefit of joining a compliance group is that when parents see that that your site has a seal of approval from one of the safe harbor programs, they'll have more confidence that their kids are in safe hands when they visit your site.

c. Getting Parental Consent

If you don't use a safe harbor program as discussed above, you'll need to design your own system for getting parental consent before you can collect personal information from a child, or from anyone if your site is directed at children. This can get complicated. The FTC requires you to make reasonable efforts to notify a parent about your information practices and get the parent's agreement. Your notice must contain the same information as in your website privacy policy. You also have to tell the parent:

- that you wish to collect information from the child
- that the parent's consent is required before you can collect, use and disclose the information, and
- how the parent can give consent.

What efforts are "reasonable" when it comes to getting the parent's consent? The requirements vary, depending on how you'll use the personal information you're trying to collect. It's easier to meet the requirements if you use the information for internal purposes only. If you disclose the information to others, tougher rules apply.

Information Used Internally. If you're only going to use the information gathered from a child for internal uses, you may obtain a parent's consent by email, if you take some precautions. By internal use, the FTC means:

- sending marketing materials to the child based on the preference or interests the child reveals to you, or
- sending promotional updates about your site.

If you do get consent by email, it's always possible that a wily child will impersonate a parent during a single session online. Therefore, the FTC requires you to take steps to increase the likelihood that the parent really did consent. This is known as *email plus*. You can get this added confirmation by letter or phone call—but it's cheaper and more efficient to get what is known as a *delayed* confirmation by email.

EXAMPLE: ProtoBiz offers to send a premium to children who visit its site. To mail the premium—an internal use of the child's information—ProtoBiz needs a child's name and address. ProtoBiz starts the process by asking the child to provide an email address for one of his or her parents. Then, ProtoBiz uses automated software to send its privacy notice and consent form to the parent's email address—and a second, similar email 12 hours later. Using this delayed confirmation method, ProtoBiz meets the FTC requirements for information that will be used internally. A sample email consent form is shown below.

Sample Form for Parent's Consent by Email

To _____:

Your child, _____, has requested a ProtoWiz Kit. Before we can send the Kit to your child, we need your consent. If you wish to consent, please complete the form below and return it us by reply email.

Thank you,

ProtoBiz

Parent's Consent:

I am a parent of _____. I have read your privacy notice. You have my permission to send your ProtoWiz Kit to my child at the following address:

_____.

_____

Name of Parent

Sample Form for Confirming Email Consent

To _____:

We recently received an email in which you appear to have consented to ProtoBiz sending a ProtoWiz Kit to your child, _____. The consent we received looks this way:

I am a parent of _____. I have read your privacy notice. You have my permission to send your ProtoWiz Kit to my child at the following address:

_____

_____

Name of Parent

Because we want to be sure we do have your permission, please click one of the boxes below, and return this to us by reply email. If you click the second box, we will consider the consent revoked.

Thank you,

ProtoBiz

❏ I confirm that the above consent is authentic.

❏ I do not grant my consent, and I revoke any prior consent you received.

Obviously, getting consent by email, even delayed email, isn't foolproof. But it's a practical system, and the FTC is comfortable with it.

Information You Disclose to Others. You may want to use personal information from children for more than internal purposes. For example, you may run a chat room or message board where you want children to know more about one another including letting them post information about where they live or go to school or what their hobbies are. Or you might want to share a child's information with another company—a third party—

with which you exchange information that can be useful in marketing to children. In these cases, you need to obtain more reliable proof of parental consent.

More reliable methods of obtaining consent include:

- getting a signed form from a parent by fax or regular mail, or
- letting parents call a toll-free number—as long as it's staffed by people trained in how to screen out kids pretending to be adults.

One of the trickier parts of the FTC rule has to do with the wording of the parent's consent when you plan to share a child's information with a third party.

If you're seeking consent to share a child's personal information with a third party, the FTC requires you to offer a parent the option of letting you collect and use the child's personal information *without* disclosing it to third parties. If the parent doesn't consent to the wider use of the information, you can share it only with those who need to know it to support operation of your website—like technical support staff—or to fulfill an order placed by the child.

Below is a sample form requesting permission for public disclosure of a child's information.

Sample Form for Parent's Consent
When Authorization for Public Disclosure Is Sought

To _____:

ProtoBiz understands that you are the parent of _____. We would like to use individually identifiable information about your child to send ProtoBiz marketing information to your child and to fulfill orders from your child. We would also like to disclose that information to third parties such as companies that may wish to send marketing information to your child.

If we have your consent, please complete the following form and fax it to us at _____ or by mail addressed to _____.

Consent:

I am a parent of _____. I have read your privacy notice. You have my permission to collect and use individually identifiable information from my child for the following purposes:

❏ Internal use only, such as sending your company's marketing information or promotional updates to my child and fulfilling orders.

❏ Internal use (as described above) *and* disclosure to third parties such as other companies that may wish to send marketing and promotional information to my child.

_____

Name of Parent

This form can be useful when you ask a parent to fax a signed consent to you. As with all forms, you need to tailor the wording to fit your situation. As a practical matter, however, using a toll-free number to get a parent's consent may be more productive. Few parents are likely to take the trouble to complete the consent form and return it by fax or mail.

Go right to the source. Since the FTC enforces the COPPA rules, we recommend that you get the compliance guidelines directly from the FTC. Visit its site at http://www.ftc.gov, click "Kidz Privacy" and read "How to Comply with the Children's Online Privacy Protection Rule." If you want to read COPPA yourself, you can find it by going to the Legal Research Center at http://www.nolo.com. Click "federal laws" and then "U.S. Code." In the "Title" box enter 15 and in the "Section" box enter 6501. COPPA is covered in sections 6501 through 6505.

3. A Sample Privacy Policy for Children

Section C above explains how to write a general privacy policy for your site. If your website is covered by COPPA, you'll want to add a section to that privacy policy concerning children. Here is a sample:

CHILDREN'S GUIDELINES

ProtoBiz follows these guidelines regarding children under 13:

We do not collect personally identifiable information without getting parental consent in advance. We give parents the opportunity to prevent use of the information and the child's participation in a website activity. Unless we have a parent's consent, we use online information only to respond to a child's request.

We do not disclose personally identifiable information to third parties or post such information on our site.

We do not use games, prizes or other activities to entice children to give more information than is needed for participation in an activity.

Let Big Bird teach you. For an example of a carefully crafted privacy policy on a website directed to children, go to http://www.sesameworkshop.org. ∎

Protecting Business Secrets

Your online business will almost certainly have some valuable information that you'd like to keep under wraps. It could be a sales plan, a customer list, a database, a system for filling orders or a software process. This confidential information is a form of property whose value would drop to zero if competitors got their hands on it. In legal terms, these are your business's *trade secrets*.

Keeping this information secret is desirable, but 100% secrecy may be impossible. You may have to share these trade secrets with employees, independent contractors and parties with whom you may be forming business relationships. To protect the confidentiality of such information, we advise using a nondisclosure agreement or NDA.

In a nondisclosure agreement, one or both parties agree to keep certain information confidential. Someone who reveals or misuses your protected information after signing a nondisclosure agreement can face serious legal sanctions. You can seek a court order barring further disclosure or misuse of the information and you can seek damages as well.

This chapter will help you identify and protect your trade secrets. Section D contains a sample nondisclosure agreement.

Information that's protected under an NDA may qualify for legal protection under copyright or patent law. For more information on nondisclosure agreements and intellectual property, read *Nondisclosure Agreements: Protecting Your Trade Secrets and More,* by Richard Stim and Stephen Fishman (Nolo).

A. Trade Secret Basics

Nondisclosure agreements won't protect just *any* business information; the information must qualify as a trade secret. Trade secrets can include such items as unpublished Web pages, business plans, financial projections, marketing plans, sales data, unpublished promotional material, cost and pricing information, customer lists, unpublished computer code, product design specifications and pending patent applications.

To qualify as a trade secret and be protected by an NDA, business information must meet three criteria:

- **The information can't be generally known or readily ascertainable.** If your competitors already know the material you want to protect, it isn't much of a secret. Once it's generally known or can be learned by the people within an industry, the information loses its special trade secret status and isn't protected by nondisclosure agreements. There's no clear line that establishes when information is "generally known" in a particular industry. In most cases, information is generally known if it's been published or publicly displayed or is commonly used within the trade. Publishing information at your website will almost always end its trade secret status. Information is "ascertainable" if it can be obtained legally within an industry—for example, if someone can find it through an online database, at a library or through other publicly available sources. A trade secret isn't readily ascertainable if bribery, fraud or other deceptive procedures are required to get it.

- **The information must provide economic value or a competitive advantage.** For most trade secrets, this requirement is easy to meet. You can show the benefits derived from your use of the trade secret or your costs of developing it, or that you've received business or licensing offers for use of the secret. A trade secret loses its economic value after it's publicly disclosed.

- **Your company must take reasonable steps to protect its trade secrets.** In general, you're considered to have taken reasonable steps if you use a sensible system for protecting information—for example, locking your

facilities, monitoring visitors and labeling confidential information.

B. How to Safeguard Trade Secrets

Here are the minimum safeguards a small online company should take to protect its trade secrets. Follow them and, if you ever need to sue to prevent someone from using or disclosing information in violation of an NDA, a judge would likely conclude that you took reasonable precautions to prevent the public or competitors from learning about your secrets.

Use NDAs. Before you give anyone access to your trade secrets, make sure that he or she has signed a nondisclosure agreement. This is the single most important element of your trade secret protection program. A basic NDA is provided in Section D.

Maintain physical security. At a minimum, documents containing trade secrets shouldn't be left on desks when not in use; rather, they should be locked in desk drawers or filing cabinets. And securely lock your office at the end of the day.

Increase computer security. Your online business likely stores most trade secrets on computer systems. To prevent unauthorized people from gaining access to the system, have employees use secret passwords and access procedures. Change your passwords periodically, especially when an employee who knows the current passwords quits or is fired. Implement a firewall—a set of software programs that protects your private network from users from other networks—to prevent trade secret theft from your company's file server. Keep trade secrets in coded or encrypted form so outsiders can't read them. Inexpensive encryption programs such as PGP (Pretty Good Privacy) are readily available. Consider using separate computer systems, without Internet or other network access, for your most sensitive information. If practical, place computers, terminals and other peripherals in a physically secure location to which access is restricted.

Label information confidential. Documents (both hard copy and electronic), software and other materials containing trade secrets should always be marked "confidential." For example, you can state: "THIS [choose one: program, document, database] IS CONFIDENTIAL AND PROPRIETARY TO [your company name] AND MAY NOT BE REPRODUCED, PUBLISHED OR DISCLOSED TO OTHERS WITHOUT COMPANY AUTHORIZATION." This is the best way to alert employees and others that a document contains trade secrets. You should also obtain a rubber stamp reading CONFIDENTIAL and use it to mark documents when it's inconvenient to use a longer notice. However, don't go overboard and mark everything in sight confidential. If virtu-

ally everything, including public information, is marked "confidential," a court may conclude that nothing was really confidential. It is better not to mark anything than to mark everything.

C. Customer Lists As Trade Secrets

One advantage of operating a business online is the ease with which you can amass and store customer data. That information is often one of your most valuable and protected assets, so consider treating your customer list and related data as a trade secret, and have employees or outside contractors sign NDAs promising not to divulge or use the information without permission. Keep in mind, however, that trade secret law won't protect every customer list.

If a dispute over a customer list ends up in court, a judge generally considers the following elements to decide whether or not it qualifies as a trade secret:

- **Is the information in the list ascertainable by other means?** For example, can someone using a search engine or email directory create a similar customer list? A list that's readily ascertainable can't be protected.
- **Does the list include more than names and email addresses?** For ex-

ample, if your customer list includes purchasing information or special needs for online customers, it's more likely to be protected because this information adds value.

- **Did it take a lot of time or effort or did you create a special system for assembling your list?** A customer list that requires more effort is more likely to be protected under an NDA.
- **Is your customer list long-standing or exclusive?** If you can prove that a customer list is special to your business and has been used for a long time, the list is more likely to be protected.

State laws prohibit employees from improper disclosure of your trade secrets even without using an NDA. It's advisable to use an NDA, however, because it may give you additional benefits if you have to sue an employee who's disclosed or misused your trade secrets. These benefits can include increased damages, payment of lawyer fees and a guarantee about where the dispute will be resolved (your headquarters state, for example) or what mechanism will be used (arbitration or a lawsuit).

D. Drafting a Nondisclosure Agreement

This section contains a basic nondisclosure agreement and an explanation of its provisions. In general, an NDA should:

- define the trade secrets
- exclude what isn't protected as a trade secret
- establish an obligation to keep the confidential information secret, and
- say how long the secrecy must be maintained.

The nondisclosure agreement in this section is an all-purpose NDA. You can use it for employees, independent contractors or companies entering into content license agreements or revenue sharing deals. If you need more specific nondisclosure agreements or more information on protecting secrets in the workplace, consult *Nondisclosure Agreements: Protecting Your Trade Secrets and More,* by Richard Stim and Stephen Fishman (Nolo).

The agreement in this chapter may be found on the CD-ROM at the back of the book.

Nondisclosure Agreement

1. Names

[ALTERNATIVE 1]

_____ (the Disclosing Party) and _____
(the Receiving Party) agree to the following terms and conditions.

[ALTERNATIVE 2]

_____ and _____ (the parties)
agree to the following terms and conditions.

Explanation: _If you're using this NDA with an employee, you should change the term_
"Receiving Party" to "Employee" and change "Disclosing Party" to "Employer."

Alternative 1 is for a "one-way" agreement in which only one party is disclosing secrets to an-
other. If both parties are disclosing secrets to each other, you should choose Alternative 2,
which creates a mutual nondisclosure agreement.

Whichever version you choose, fill in the appropriate names. See Chapter 3, Section E, for in-
formation on inserting names into contracts.

2. Purpose

[ALTERNATIVE 1]

The Disclosing Party may disclose Confidential Information to the Receiving Party in pursuing or establishing a business relationship or negotiating a contract between the parties.
This Agreement is intended to prevent the unauthorized disclosure of that Confidential Information.

[ALTERNATIVE 2]

One party (the Disclosing Party) may disclose Confidential Information to the other party
(the Receiving Party). By this Agreement, the parties are creating a mutual confidential relationship to prevent unauthorized disclosure of the Confidential Information.

Explanation: _This clause establishes the general nature of the agreement. Use Alternate 1_
for a "one-way" agreement. Use Alternative 2 for a mutual agreement.

3. Confidential Information

[ALTERNATIVE 1]

Receiving Party acknowledges that the following information constitutes confidential proprietary trade secret information (Confidential Information) belonging to Disclosing Party:

[ALTERNATIVE 2]

Receiving Party acknowledges that Disclosing Party's confidential proprietary trade secret information (Confidential Information) consists of information and materials that are valuable and not generally known by Disclosing Party's competitors. Confidential Information includes:

(a) Information concerning Disclosing Party's current, future or proposed products, including, but not limited to, formulas, designs, devices, computer code, drawings, specifications, notebook entries, technical notes and graphs, computer printouts, technical memoranda and correspondence, product development agreements and related agreements.

(b) Information and materials relating to Disclosing Party's purchasing, accounting and marketing, including, but not limited to, marketing plans, sales data, business methods, unpublished promotional material, cost and pricing information and customer lists.

(c) Information of the type described above which Disclosing Party obtained from another party and which Disclosing Party treats as confidential, whether or not owned or developed by Disclosing Party.

(d) Other: _____

Explanation: *Select either Alternative 1 or 2, and delete the other. Here's how to choose:*

Alternative 1. It's best to specifically identify the trade secrets covered by the agreement; use this clause if you can individually list the material being provided. However, be careful that your description is not so narrowly worded that it may leave out important information you wish to have covered by the agreement.

Alternative 2. Use this clause if you can't specifically identify the trade secrets—for example, if the information to be disclosed doesn't yet exist when the agreement is signed. This clause contains a general description of the types of information covered.

4. Nondisclosure

In consideration of Disclosing Party's disclosure of its Confidential Information to Receiving Party, Receiving Party agrees that it will treat Disclosing Party's Confidential Information with the same degree of care and safeguards that it takes with its own Confidential Information, and with at least a reasonable degree of care. Receiving Party agrees that, without Disclosing Party's prior written consent, Receiving Party will not:

(a) disclose Disclosing Party's Confidential Information to any third party;

(b) make or permit to be made copies or other reproductions of Disclosing Party's Confidential Information; or

(c) make any commercial use of the Confidential Information.

Receiving Party will carefully restrict access to the Confidential Information to those of its officers, directors and employees who clearly need such access to participate on Receiving Party's behalf in the analysis and negotiation of a business relationship or any contract or agreement with Disclosing Party.

Receiving Party will advise each officer, director or employee to whom it provides access to any of the Confidential Information that they are prohibited from using it or disclosing it to others without the Disclosing Party's prior written consent.

[OPTIONAL]

In addition, without prior written consent of Disclosing Party, Receiving Party will not disclose to any person either the fact that discussions or negotiations are taking place concerning a possible transaction or the status of such discussions or negotiations.

Explanation: *This clause makes clear that the trade secrets must be kept in confidence by the receiving party and may not be revealed to others without the disclosing party's prior written consent. It contains an optional provision requiring the fact that negotiations are taking place to be kept secret.*

5. Return of Materials

Upon Disclosing Party's request, Receiving Party will within 30 days return all original materials provided by Disclosing Party and any copies, notes or other documents in Receiving Party's possession pertaining to Disclosing Party's Confidential Information.

Explanation: *In this clause, the receiving party promises to return original materials provided by the disclosing party, as well as copies, notes and documents pertaining to the trade secrets. The form gives the receiving party 30 days to return the materials, but you can change this time period if you wish.*

6. Exclusions

This agreement does not apply to any information which:

(a) was in Receiving Party's possession or was known to Receiving Party, without an obligation to keep it confidential, before such information was disclosed to Receiving Party by Disclosing Party;

(b) is or becomes public knowledge through a source other than Receiving Party and through no fault of Receiving Party;

(c) is or becomes lawfully available to Receiving Party from a source other than Disclosing Party; or

(d) is disclosed by Receiving Party with Disclosing Party's prior written approval.

Explanation: *This provision describes all the types of information that are not covered by the agreement. These exclusions are based on court decisions and state trade secret laws that hold that these types of information don't qualify for trade secret protection.*

7. Term

[ALTERNATIVE 1]

This Agreement and Receiving Party's duty to hold Disclosing Party's trade secrets in confidence will continue until the Confidential Information is no longer a trade secret or until Disclosing Party sends Receiving Party written notice releasing Receiving Party from this Agreement, whichever occurs first.

[ALTERNATIVE 2]

This Agreement and Receiving Party's duty to hold Disclosing Party's Confidential Information in confidence will continue until _____ or until whichever of the following occurs first:

(a) the Disclosing Party sends the Receiving Party written notice releasing it from this Agreement, or

(b) the Confidential Information ceases to be a trade secret.

Explanation: *There are two alternative provisions dealing with the agreement's term. Select the clause that best suits your needs and delete the other.*

Alternative 1. This provision has no definite time limit—in other words, the receiving party's obligation of confidentiality lasts until the trade secret information ceases to be a trade secret. This may occur when the information becomes generally known, is disclosed to the public by the disclosing party or ceases being a trade secret for some other reason. This gives the disclosing party the broadest protection possible.

Alternative 2. Some receiving parties don't want to be subject to open-ended confidentiality obligations. Use this clause if the receiving party requires that the agreement provide a definite date in which the agreement, and the receiving party's confidentiality obligations, expires. The agreement should last as long as the information is likely to remain a trade secret. Five years is a common time period, but the period can be much shorter, even as little as six months. In Internet and technology businesses, the time period may need to be shorter because of the fast pace of innovation.

8. No Rights Granted

This Agreement does not constitute a grant or an intention or commitment to grant any right, title or interest in disclosing party's Confidential Information to Receiving Party.

Explanation: *This clause makes clear that the disclosing party isn't granting any ownership rights in the confidential information to the receiving party.*

9. Injunctive Relief

Any breach or threatened breach of this Agreement by Receiving Party may cause Disclosing Party irreparable harm for which monetary damages may be inadequate. Disclosing Party will be entitled to an injunction to restrain Receiving Party from such breach or threatened breach. Nothing in this Agreement will prevent Disclosing Party from pursuing any remedy at law or in equity for any breach or threatened breach of this Agreement.

Explanation: *One of the most important legal remedies a trade secret owner can obtain if someone violates a nondisclosure agreement is a court order preventing the violator from using or profiting from the trade secrets. This provision is intended to make such a court order—called an injunction—easier to obtain. Some parties may object to inclusion of this provision because they want to make it as hard as possible for the other side to obtain an injunction.*

10. Invalid Provisions

If a court finds any provision of this Agreement invalid or unenforceable, the remainder of this Agreement will be interpreted so as best to carry out the parties' intent.

Explanation: *Clauses like those in sections 10 through 16 are found in many types of agreements. For more information, see Chapter 3.*

11. Entire Agreement

This is the entire Agreement between the parties. It replaces and supersedes any oral agreements between the parties, as well as any prior writings.

12. Modification

Any modifications to this Agreement must be in writing.

13. Waiver

The failure to exercise any right in this Agreement will not waive prior or subsequent rights.

14. Successors and Assigns

This agreement binds and benefits the heirs, successors and assigns of the parties.

15. Attorney Fees and Expenses

If there is litigation, the prevailing party may collect from the other party its reasonable costs and attorney fees incurred in enforcing this Agreement.

16. Governing Law

This Agreement will be governed by and construed in accordance with the laws of the state of _____.

Dated: _____

DISCLOSING PARTY

Name of Business: _____

A _____

By_____

Printed Name and Title: _____

Address: _____

_____

RECEIVING PARTY

Name of Business: _____

A _____

By _____

Printed Name and Title: _____

Address: _____

_____

Explanation: *Each party should sign at least two copies, and keep at least one so that both parties have an original signed agreement. See Chapter 3, Section E4, for information on signing contracts.*

Noncompete Agreements— When an NDA Isn't Enough

A noncompetition agreement (also called a *noncompete* or *covenant not to compete*) is a contract in which someone agrees not to compete with your company for a certain period of time. Noncompetition and nondisclosure agreements both have the same goal: to prevent a competitor from using valuable business information. The difference is that a noncompete is broader; it prohibits even working for a competitor or starting a competing business. The restrictions are so heavy-handed that some states refuse to enforce (or limit enforcement of) them.

For more information on noncompete agreements, consult *How to Create a Noncompete Agreement,* by Shannon Miehe (Nolo). ■

Because courts are averse to enforcing them and employees dislike being asked to sign them, noncompete agreements are a potential minefield. In addition, there's a growing body of public information that helps employees break noncompete agreements (for example, http://www.breakyournoncompete.com). Before entering into a noncompete with an employee, learn the law in your state and speak with an attorney.

Lawyers and Legal Research

When you own or run a small business, you need lots of legal information. Lawyers, of course, are prime sources of this information, but if you bought all you needed at their rates—$150 to $350 an hour—you'd quickly empty your bank account. Fortunately, there are a number of efficient ways you can acquire on your own a good working knowledge of the important legal principles and procedures.

But can you create and run your Web business without ever consulting a lawyer? Probably not. Lawyers do more than dispense legal information. They also offer strategic advice and apply sophisticated technical skills. How frequently you'll need professional help is hard to say. It depends on the nature of your business, the number of employees you hire, how many locations you have and the kinds of problems you run into with customers, suppliers, landlords, contractors, the government, the media, insurance companies and a host of other people and entities. Your challenge isn't to avoid lawyers altogether but rather to use them on a cost-effective basis.

Ideally, you should find a lawyer who's willing to serve as a legal coach and help you educate yourself. Then you can negotiate many legal transactions on your own and prepare preliminary drafts of documents, turning to your lawyer from time to time for advice, review and fine-tuning.

When you work with a lawyer, you're the boss. A lawyer, of course, has specialized training, knowledge, skill and experience in dealing with legal matters. But that's no reason for you to abdicate control over decision-making and how much time and money should be spent on a particular legal problem. Because you almost surely can't afford all the legal services that you'd benefit from, you need to set priorities. When thinking about a legal problem, ask yourself whether you can handle it yourself, handle it with some help from a lawyer, or if you should simply put it in your lawyer's hands.

> ### How a Business Lawyer Can Help You With Your Web Business
>
> - Assist with the start-up of your online business—for example, help you decide whether to set up a separate legal entity for your online activities.
> - Look over a proposed lease for your online business's office space.
> - Review agreements to guarantee your ownership of materials created for your website.
> - Represent you at the Patent and Trademark Office or assist you with issues concerning domain names, copyrights and trade secrets.
> - Coach or represent you in lawsuits or arbitrations where the stakes are high or the legal issues complex.
> - Review or draft documents when you buy or sell a business, license content or enter into agreements with other businesses.

A. How to Find the Right Lawyer

Locating a good lawyer for your online business may not be as easy as you think. Of the close to 650,000 practicing lawyers in America today, probably fewer than 50,000 possess adequate training and experience in small business law. And of that group, many lack in-depth experience in working for Web businesses.

1. What Not to Do

Don't expect to locate a good business lawyer by simply looking in the phone book, consulting a law directory or reading an advertisement. There's not enough information in these sources to help you make a valid judgment. Almost as useless are lawyer referral services operated by bar associations. Generally, these services make little attempt to evaluate a lawyer's skill and experience. They simply supply the names of lawyers who have signed up with the service, often accepting the lawyer's own word about skills and experience.

2. Compiling a List of Prospects

A better approach is to talk to people in your community who own or operate successful Web businesses. If you talk to half a dozen business people, chances are you'll come away with several good leads.

Other people who provide services to the business community can also help you. Ask them specifically about lawyers who have experience working for Web business clients. Here are a few other sources you can turn to for possible candidates:

- the director of your state or local chamber of commerce
- a law librarian can help identify authors in your state who have written

books or articles on online business law, or

- the director of your state's continuing legal education (CLE) program—usually run by a bar association, a law school or both—can identify lawyers who lecture or write on Internet business law for other lawyers. Someone who's a "lawyer's lawyer" presumably has the depth of knowledge and experience to do a superior job for you—but may charge accordingly.

Once you have the names of several lawyers, a good source of more information about them is the Martindale-Hubbell Law Directory, available online at most law libraries and some local public libraries. This resource contains biographical sketches of most practicing lawyers and information about their experience, specialties, education and the professional organizations they belong to. Many firms also list their major clients in the directory—an excellent indication of the types of practice the firm is engaged in.

In addition, almost every lawyer listed in the directory is rated "AV," "BV" or "CV." These ratings come from confidential opinions that Martindale-Hubbell solicits from lawyers and judges. The first letter is for "Legal Ability," which is rated as follows:

- "A"—Very High to Preeminent
- "B"—High to Very High
- "C"—Fair to High

The "V" part stands for "Very High General Recommendation," meaning that the rated lawyer adheres to professional standards of conduct and ethics. But it's practically meaningless because lawyers who don't qualify for it aren't rated at all.

(Martindale-Hubbell prudently cautions that the absence of a rating shouldn't be construed as a reflection on the lawyer; some lawyers ask that their rating not be published, and there may be other reasons for the absence of a rating.)

The rating system works remarkably well. Don't make it your sole criterion for deciding on a potential lawyer for your business, but be reasonably confident that a lawyer who gets high marks from other business clients and an "AV" rating from Martindale-Hubbell knows what he or she is doing.

You can reach Martindale-Hubbell online at http://www.martindale.com. The hardcover books are available at many law libraries.

Another source of information about lawyers is the West Legal Directory at http://www.lawoffice.com. This online service allows users to search by legal specialty, law firm, lawyer name or by city.

3. Shopping Around

After you get the names of several good prospects, shop around. If you announce your intentions in advance, most lawyers will be willing to speak to you for a half hour or so at no charge so that you can size them up and make an informed decision. Look for experience, personal rapport and accessibility. Some of these characteristics will be apparent almost immediately. Others may take longer to discover. So even after you've hired a lawyer who seems right for you, keep open the possibility that you may have to make a change later.

Pay particular attention to the rapport between you and your lawyer. No matter how experienced and well-recommended a lawyer is, if you feel uncomfortable during your first meeting or two, you may never achieve a good lawyer-client relationship. Trust your instincts and seek a lawyer whose personality is compatible with your own.

Your lawyer should be accessible when you need legal services. Unfortunately, probably the most common complaint about lawyers is that they don't return clients' phone calls quickly enough. If every time you have a problem there's a delay of several days before you can talk to your lawyer on the phone or get an appointment, you'll lose precious time, not to mention sleep. And almost nothing is more aggravating to a client than to leave a legal project in a lawyer's hands and then have weeks or even months go by without anything happening. You want a lawyer who will work hard on your behalf and follow through promptly on all assignments.

Try to find a lawyer who seems interested in your Web business and either already knows a lot about your field or who seems genuinely eager to learn more about it. Avoid the lawyer who's aloof and doesn't want to get involved in learning the nitty-gritty details of what you do.

Some lawyers are nitpickers who get unnecessarily bogged down in legal minutiae while a valuable business opportunity slips away. You want a lawyer who blends sound legal advice with a practical approach—someone who figures out a way to do something, not one who only offers reasons why it can't be done.

B. Fees and Bills

When you hire a lawyer, get a clear understanding about how fees will be computed. And as new jobs are brought to the lawyer, ask specifically about charges for each. Many lawyers initiate fee discussions, but others forget or are shy about doing so. Bring up the subject yourself. Insist that the ground rules be clearly established. In California, all fee agreements between lawyers and clients must be in writing if the expected fee is $1,000 or more, or is contingent on the outcome of a lawsuit. In any state, it's a good idea.

1. How Lawyers Charge

There are four basic ways that lawyers charge. The first is by the hour. In most parts of the United States, you can get competent services for your small business for $150 to $250 an hour.

The cheapest hourly rate isn't necessarily the best deal. A novice who charges only $80 an hour may take three hours to review a consultant's work-for-hire contract. A more experienced lawyer who charges $200 an hour may do the same job in half an hour and make better suggestions. Take into account the lawyer's knowledge, reputation and the personal rapport the two of you have—or don't have.

Sometimes a lawyer quotes a flat fee for a specific job. For example, the lawyer may offer to draw up a nondisclosure agreement for $300, or review and edit your customer policies (terms and conditions) for $500. You pay the same amount regardless of how much time the lawyer spends.

In some cases, a lawyer may charge a contingent fee. This is a percentage (commonly 33%) of the amount the lawyer obtains for you in a negotiated settlement or through a trial. If the lawyer recovers nothing for you, there's no fee. However, the lawyer does generally expect reimbursement for out-of-pocket expenses, such as filing fees, long distance phone calls and transcripts of testimony. Contingent fees are common in personal injury lawsuits but relatively unusual in small business matters.

Finally, you may be able to hire a lawyer for a flat annual fee (retainer) to handle all of your routine legal business. You'll usually pay in equal monthly installments and, normally, the lawyer will bill you an additional amount for extraordinary services—such as representing you in a major lawsuit. Obviously, the key to making this arrangement work is to have a written agreement clearly defining what's routine and what's extraordinary.

2. Ways to Save on Legal Fees

There are many ways to hold down the cost of legal services. Here's a summary.

Group together your legal affairs. You'll save money if you consult with your lawyer on several matters at one time. For example, in a one-hour conference, you may be able to review the annual updating of your corporate record book, renewing your Web hosting agreement and a noncompetition agreement you've drafted for new employees to sign.

Help out. You or your employees can do a lot of work yourselves. Help gather documents needed for a transaction. Write the first couple of drafts of a contract; give your lawyer the relatively inexpensive task of reviewing and polishing the document.

Ask the lawyer to be your coach.
Make it clear that you're eager to do as much work as possible yourself with the lawyer coaching you from the sidelines. For example, if you are involved in a domain name dispute, you may file arbitration papers, do research and prepare your own papers—all with your attorney looking over your shoulder, guiding your work. Many lawyers are used to clients who simply drop their problems on the lawyer's desk to solve. Unless you specifically ask for coaching, you may never tap into your lawyer's ability to help you in that way.

Educate yourself. In Section D, you'll find many sources of legal information on the Web. These sites will help you keep up with specific legal developments that your lawyer may have missed. Send pertinent articles to your lawyer—this can dramatically reduce legal research time—and encourage your lawyer to do the same for you.

Show that you're an important client. The single most important thing you can do to tell your lawyer how much you value the relationship is to pay your bills on time. Also, let your lawyer know about plans for expansion and your company's possible future legal needs. And if your business wins an award or otherwise is recognized as being a leader in its field, let your lawyer know about it—everyone feels good when an enterprise they're associated with prospers.

Also, let your lawyer know when you recommend him or her to business colleagues.

Use other professionals. Often, non-lawyer professionals perform some tasks better and at less cost than lawyers do. For example, look to management consultants for strategic business planning; real estate brokers or appraisers for valuation of properties; accountants for preparation of financial proposals; insurance agents for advice on insurance protection; and CPAs for the preparation of tax returns.

Keep business and personal bills separate. If you visit your lawyer on a personal legal matter and you also discuss a business problem, ask your lawyer to allocate the time spent and send you separate bills. At tax time, you can easily list the business portion as a tax-deductible business expense.

C. Problems With Your Lawyer

Relations between lawyers and clients are not always perfect. If you see a problem emerging, don't just sit back and fume; call, visit or write to your lawyer. The problem won't get resolved if your lawyer doesn't even know there's a problem. Sure, it's hard to confront someone whom you may need to rely on for future help and advice—but an open exchange is essential for a healthy lawyer-client relationship.

Whatever it is that rankles, have an honest discussion about your feelings. Maybe you're upset because your lawyer hasn't kept you informed about what's going on in your case or has failed to meet a promised deadline. Or maybe last month's bill was shockingly high or lacked any breakdown of how your lawyer's time was spent.

One good test of whether a lawyer-client relationship is a good one is to ask yourself if you feel able to talk freely with your lawyer about your degree of participation in any legal matter and your control over how the lawyer carries out an assignment. If you can't frankly discuss these sometimes sensitive matters with your lawyer, get another lawyer. Otherwise, you'll surely waste money on unnecessary legal fees and risk having legal matters turn out badly. Remember that you're always free to change lawyers and to get all important documents back from a lawyer you no longer employ.

Your Rights As a Client

The following rules are not written into law, but we recommend them as guidelines. A client has the right:

1. To be treated courteously by the lawyer and staff members.
2. To receive an itemized statement of services rendered and a full explanation of billing practices.
3. To be charged reasonable fees.
4. To receive a prompt response to phone calls and letters.
5. To have confidential legal conferences, free from unwarranted interruptions.
6. To be kept informed of the status of the case.
7. To have your legal matters handled diligently and competently.
8. To receive clear answers to all questions.

For more information about dealing with attorneys, look at *The Lawsuit Survival Guide* (Nolo), by attorney Joe Matthews, or *Mad at Your Lawyer*, a downloadable eGuide by attorney Tanya Starnes, that is available at the Nolo website.

D. Do-it-Yourself Legal Research

The Internet and local law libraries are chock full of valuable information that you can easily ferret out on your own. All you need is a rudimentary knowledge of how the information is organized.

1. Online Research

Online research is speedy and inexpensive. Be sure to stop at Nolo's own site, http://www.nolo.com, where you'll discover loads of material on Internet and small business law as well as legal research links.

For an introduction to the vast amount of cyber-info that's out there, you might sample these sites:

- Gigalaw.Com at http:// www.gigalaw.com is a good source of Internet law. Its daily email alerts (you can subscribe at the site's home page) are one of the best sources for changes in online business law.
- *The Internet Law Journal* (http:// www.tilj.com) offers an email service as well as a collection of articles on Internet law.
- *Lawyers Weekly* at http:// www.lweekly.com has up-to-date news on a wide range of legal topics. Check out the aptly named Treasure Chest of Important Documents for items you might want to download.

- Martindale-Hubbell at http:// www.lawyers.com contains very helpful features as well as lawyer listings. For example, by clicking "Ask a Lawyer," you can pose a question of general interest and receive an online answer from a practitioner on Martindale-Hubbell's panel. The Law Today area has information on current legal topics.
- The "legal portal" at http:// www.law.com has separate areas for the public, businesses, lawyers and students.
- The Thomas Legislative Information site (named after Thomas Jefferson) at http://thomas.loc.gov contains a wealth of information on bills pending in Congress and laws recently adopted.
- The Court TV Small Business Law Center at http://www.courttv.com/ legalhelp/business offers articles on small business law and also provides some legal forms.
- Lectric Law Library at http:// www.lectlaw.com is a good place to explore a wide range of business law issues. Many business law topics are covered in reasonable depth.
- The Internal Revenue Service at http:// www.irs.gov lets you download tax forms, instructions and a wide range of IRS publications.
- BizLaw e-zine at http:// www.biztalk.com contains legal infor-

mation for starting and expanding a business. Look for the *bizlaw* part of the site.

- National Federation of Independent Business at http://www.nfibonline.com is a good place to check on small business news and get practical tips.
- U.S. Small Business Administration at http://www.sbaonline.sba.gov features information on starting and financing your small business.
- CCH Incorporated at http://www.cch.com provides current legal information on federal and state tax law, financial law, corporate law and legal issues relevant to small business owners.

2. Law Libraries

You can also conduct thorough legal research at your local law library. Your first step is to find a law library that's open to the public. You may find one in your county courthouse or at your state capi-

tol. Public law schools generally permit the public to use their libraries, and some private law schools grant access to their libraries—sometimes for a modest user fee. The reference department of a major public library may have a fairly decent legal research collection. If you're lucky enough to have access to several law libraries, select one that has a reference librarian to assist you.

Finally, don't overlook the law library in your own lawyer's office. Most lawyers, if you ask, will gladly share their books.

Legal Research: How to Find and Understand the Law, by Stephen Elias and Susan Levinkind (Nolo), is a nontechnical book written for the average person. It covers basic legal materials, and explains how to use all major legal research tools. It's a helpful resource for framing your research questions—not always an intuitive activity. ■

Appendix

Appendix: How to Use the CD-ROM

The forms discussed in this book are included on a CD-ROM in the back of the book. This CD-ROM, which can be used with Windows computers, installs files that can be opened, printed and edited using a word processor or other software. It is *not* a stand-alone software program. Please read this Appendix and the README.TXT file included on the CD-ROM for instructions on using the Forms CD.

Note to Mac users: This CD-ROM and its files should also work on Macintosh computers. Please note, however, that Nolo cannot provide technical support for non-Windows users.

How to View the README File

If you do not know how to view the file README.TXT, insert the Forms CD-ROM into your computer's CD-ROM drive and follow these instructions:

- Windows 9x, 2000 and ME: (1) On your PC's desktop, double-click the My Computer icon; (2) double-click the icon for the CD-ROM drive into which the Forms CD-ROM was inserted; (3) double-click the file README.TXT.
- Macintosh: (1) On your Mac desktop, double-click the icon for the CD-ROM that you inserted; (2) double-click on the file README.TXT.

    While the README file is open, print it out by using the Print command in the File menu.

A. Installing the Form Files Onto Your Computer

Word processing forms that you can open, complete, print and save with your word processing program (see Section B, below) are contained on the CD-ROM. Before you can do anything with the files on the CD-ROM, you need to install them onto your hard disk. In accordance with U.S. copyright laws, remember that copies of the CD-ROM and its files are for your personal use only.

Insert the Forms CD and do the following:

1. Windows 9x, 2000 and ME Users

Follow the instructions that appear on the screen. (If nothing happens when you insert the Forms CD-ROM, then (1) double-click the My Computer icon; (2) double-click the icon for the CD-ROM drive into which the Forms CD-ROM was inserted; and (3) double-click the file WELCOME.EXE.)

By default, all the files are installed to the \Web Business Forms folder in the \Program Files folder of your computer. A folder called "Web Business Forms" is added to the "Programs" folder of the Start menu.

2. Macintosh Users

Step 1: If the "Web Business Forms CD" window is not open, open it by double-clicking the "Web Business Forms CD" icon.

Step 2: Select the "Web Business Forms" folder icon.

Step 3: Drag and drop the folder icon onto the icon of your hard disk.

B. Using the Word Processing Files to Create Documents

This section concerns the files for forms that can be opened and edited with your word processing program.

All word processing forms come in rich text format. These files have the extension ".RTF." For example, the form for the Website Development Agreement discussed in Chapter 3 is on the file Web Dev Agrmnt.RTF. All forms and their filenames are listed in Section C, below.

RTF files can be read by most recent word processing programs, including all versions of MS Word for Windows and Macintosh, WordPad for Windows, and recent versions of WordPerfect for Windows and Macintosh.

To use a form from the CD to create your documents you must: (1) open a file in your word processor or text editor; (2) edit the form by filling in the required information; (3) print it out; (4) rename and save your revised file.

The following are general instructions on how to do this. However, each word processor uses different commands to open, format, save and print documents. Please read your word processor's manual for specific instructions on performing these tasks.

Do not call Nolo's technical support if you have questions on how to use your word processor.

Step 1: Opening a File

There are three ways to open the word processing files included on the CD-ROM after you have installed them onto your computer.

- Windows users can open a file by selecting its "shortcut" as follows: (1) Click the Windows "Start" button; (2) open the "Programs" folder; (3) open the "Web Business Forms" subfolder; and (4) click on the shortcut to the form you want to work with.
- Both Windows and Macintosh users can open a file directly by double-clicking on it. Use My Computer or Windows Explorer (Windows 9x, 2000 or ME) or the Finder (Macintosh) to go to the folder you installed or copied the CD-ROM's files to. Then, double-click on the specific file you want to open.
- You can also open a file from within your word processor. To do this, you must first start your word processor. Then, go to the File menu and choose the Open command. This opens a dialog box where you will tell the program (1) the type of file you want to open (*.RTF); and (2) the location and name of the file (you will need to navigate through the directory tree to get to the folder on your hard disk where the CD's files have been installed). If these directions are unclear you will need to

look through the manual for your word processing program—Nolo's technical support department will *not* be able to help you with the use of your word processing program.

Where Are the Files Installed?

Windows Users

- RTF files are installed by default to a folder named \Web Business Forms in the \Program Files folder of your computer.

Macintosh Users

- RTF files are located in the "Web Business Forms" folder.

Step 2: Editing Your Document

Fill in the appropriate information according to the instructions and sample agreements in the book. Underlines are used to indicate where you need to enter your information, frequently followed by instructions in brackets. *Be sure to delete the underlines and instructions from your edited document.* If you do not know how to use your word processor to edit a document, you will need to look through the manual for your word processing program—Nolo's technical support department will *not* be able to help you with the use of your word processing program.

Editing Forms That Have Optional or Alternative Text

Some of the forms have check boxes before text. The check boxes indicate:

- Optional text, where you choose whether to include or exclude the given text.
- Alternative text, where you select one alternative to include and exclude the other alternatives.

We recommend that instead of marking the check boxes, you do the following:

Optional text

If you don't want to include optional text, just delete it from your document.

If you do want to include optional text, just leave it in your document.

In either case, delete the check box itself as well as the italicized instructions that the text is optional.

NOTE: If you choose not to include an optional numbered clause, be sure to renumber all the subsequent clauses after you delete it.

Alternative text

First delete all the alternatives that you do not want to include.

Then delete the remaining check boxes, as well as the italicized instructions that you need to select one of the alternatives provided.

Step 3: Printing Out the Document

Use your word processor's or text editor's "Print" command to print out your document. If you do not know how to use your word processor to print a document, you will need to look through the manual for your word processing program—Nolo's technical support department will *not* be able to help you with the use of your word processing program.

Step 4: Saving Your Document

After filling in the form, use the "Save As" command to save and rename the file. Because all the files are "read-only," you will not be able to use the "Save" command. This is for your protection. *If you save the file without renaming it, the underlines that indicate where you need to enter your information will be lost and you will not be able to create a new document with this file without recopying the original file from the CD-ROM.*

If you do not know how to use your word processor to save a document, you will need to look through the manual for your word processing program—Nolo's technical support department will *not* be able to help you with the use of your word processing program.

C. Forms Included on the Forms CD

File Name	Form Title
Affiliate Agrmnt.RTF	Affiliate Agreement
Content Agrmnt.RTF	Content License Agreement
COPPA Notices.RTF	COPPA Notices
Assignment.RTF	Copyright Assignment
Work For Hire.RTF	Language for Work for Hire Agreement
Linking Agrmnt.RTF	Linking Agreement
Nondisclosure.RTF	Nondisclosure Agreement
1st Delay.RTF	Notice of Delay: First Notice
No Date Delay.RTF	Notice of Delay: No New Shipping Date
COPPA Policy.RTF	Privacy Policy for Children
Privacy.RTF	Privacy Policy
Web Dev Agrmnt.RTF	Website Development Agreement
Policies.RTF	Website Policies ■

Index

Take 2 minutes & Give us your 2 cents

Your comments make a big difference in the development and revision of Nolo books and software. Please take a few minutes and register your Nolo product—and your comments—with us. Not only will your input make a difference, you'll receive special offers available only to registered owners of Nolo products on our newest books and software. Register now by:

PHONE
1-800-728-3555

FAX
1-800-645-0895

EMAIL
cs@nolo.com

or **MAIL** us
this registration card

REMEMBER:
Little publishers have big ears. We really listen to you.

fold here

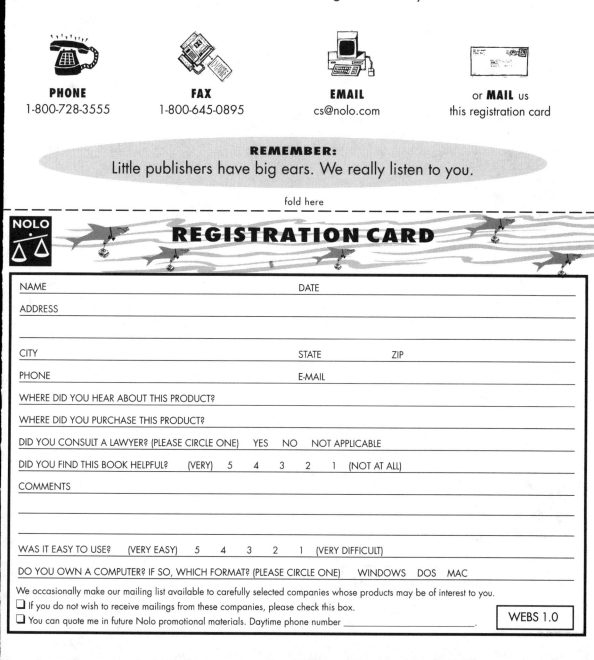

REGISTRATION CARD

NAME		DATE	
ADDRESS			

CITY		STATE	ZIP
PHONE		E-MAIL	

WHERE DID YOU HEAR ABOUT THIS PRODUCT?

WHERE DID YOU PURCHASE THIS PRODUCT?

DID YOU CONSULT A LAWYER? (PLEASE CIRCLE ONE)   YES   NO   NOT APPLICABLE

DID YOU FIND THIS BOOK HELPFUL?   (VERY)   5   4   3   2   1   (NOT AT ALL)

COMMENTS

WAS IT EASY TO USE?   (VERY EASY)   5   4   3   2   1   (VERY DIFFICULT)

DO YOU OWN A COMPUTER? IF SO, WHICH FORMAT? (PLEASE CIRCLE ONE)   WINDOWS   DOS   MAC

We occasionally make our mailing list available to carefully selected companies whose products may be of interest to you.
❏ If you do not wish to receive mailings from these companies, please check this box.
❏ You can quote me in future Nolo promotional materials. Daytime phone number _____.

WEBS 1.0

NOLO IN THE NEWS

"Nolo helps lay people perform legal tasks without the aid—or fees—of lawyers."

—USA TODAY

Nolo books are ..."written in plain language, free of legal mumbo jumbo, and spiced with witty personal observations."

—ASSOCIATED PRESS

"...Nolo publications...guide people simply through the how, when, where and why of law."

—WASHINGTON POST

"Increasingly, people who are not lawyers are performing tasks usually regarded as legal work... And consumers, using books like Nolo's, do routine legal work themselves."

—NEW YORK TIMES

"...All of [Nolo's] books are easy-to-understand, are updated regularly, provide pull-out forms...and are often quite moving in their sense of compassion for the struggles of the lay reader."

—SAN FRANCISCO CHRONICLE

fold here

Place
stamp here

nolo

950 Parker Street
Berkeley, CA 94710-9867

Attn: | **WEBS 1.0**